Star Turns

Other Books by F. W. Thomas:

Extra Turns (1917)
Saturday Nights (1923)
Low and I: A Cooked Tour in London (1923)
Merry Go Round (1924)
Rain and Shine (1924)
Cobbler's Wax (1925)
The Low and I Holiday Book (1925)
Week-Ends (1925)
All A-Blowing (1927)
Windfalls (1932)
The Merrygo Almanack (1933)
The Ballads of Barnacle Bill and Other Jingles (1943)
The Story of Searchlight (1954)
Tales From Stonecutter Street (2010)

Star Turns

F. W. Thomas

Edited by Richard Simms

Richard Simms Publications

This paperback first edition published in 2011

Richard Simms Publications, Surrey, England

ISBN: 978-0-9556942-7-1

The articles and sketches in this collection were originally published in *The Star* newspaper from 1912 to 1913.

The cover illustration is a reproduction of the original *Star* masthead, as it appeared on the front page of the newspaper for many years.

With special thanks to Morgan Wallace, Robin Andrews, David Andrews and Wendy Marriott.

For more information please visit the F. W. Thomas web page:

http://thestarfictionindex.atwebpages.com/f_w.htm

Contents

Introduction

F. W. Thomas began his journalistic career in 1905 when, after a period of unemployment, he found himself a job working as a clerk on the staff of the *Morning Leader*, a newspaper whose offices were situated in Stonecutter Street, a stone's throw from Fleet Street in central London. Shortly before securing employment with the paper, Thomas had successfully contributed three memorable articles to its editor, Ernest Parke. With the newspaper quickly promoting him to the status of reporter, Thomas soon found himself writing more articles and sketches for Parke, who greatly encouraged the young journalist to develop his embryonic humorous style. Thomas' entire output for the *Morning Leader* has now been assembled in book form in the collection *Tales From Stonecutter Street* (2010).

His association with the *Morning Leader* came to an end when in May of 1912 the Cadbury family bought it and its sister publication, the London evening newspaper *The Star*. Along with Ernest Parke, Thomas joined his new employers at their headquarters in nearby Bouverie Street. The *Leader* having been merged with the *Daily News* (for which newly amalgamated paper he was to write regularly in the years to come), Thomas shortly thereafter switched his services to *The Star*. He was to remain with the title for over thirty years.

The book you are holding in your hands is a selection of some of the best of Thomas' sketches for *The Star*, published during his first two years with the paper, 1912 and 1913. As an aside, I would like to note here that, after carefully assessing all his work from this period, I found the general level of quality to be high, thus making it difficult to find all that many pieces to exclude from this collection. And so, the result of deeming most of them worthy of another airing all these years later is a much larger anthology than I'd anticipated!

One further observation that may be of interest to the inquiring reader is that Thomas' early years with *The Star* provided much of the material for his first hardbound collection, the best-selling *Extra Turns*, published in 1917. To avoid duplication, I have elected not to include here any of the sketches from 1912 to 1913 that were reprinted in that book. If you enjoy the pieces I have gathered together here, then for more of the same I can heartily recommend to you *Extra Turns*. Reprinted several times, at the time of writing used copies are still easy enough to pick up on the Internet.

On August 14, 1912, *The Star* printed Thomas' first feature article for the paper. "Bed and Breakfast," and indeed others published in *The Star* through November 1912, read as outtakes from his spell with the *Morning Leader*. Unrepresentative of his later work, at this time Thomas was writing at about pretty much whatever subject took his fancy. Whether sharing his experience of rural inns, or waxing lyrical when detailing his almost obsessive appreciation for muffins, the author invites the reader to share in his likes.

Or, in some cases, his dislikes. Take " 'This Style'," for example, wherein Thomas gives vent to his indignation over shop mannequins (of all things!). Owning up to a profound dislike of these travesties of humanity, he attempts to reason it out, providing his audience with much to chuckle over. Then there is "The 'Wow-Wow'," in which Thomas shakes his head at a strange verbal expression that has become popular with certain sections of London youth. I admit this particular article caused me to scratch my head a bit, but notwithstanding that, it does give us an insight into the author's character and also exhibits flashes of his wry sense of humour.

In summary, these initial articles for *The Star*, penned in the summer and autumn of 1912, provide us with a convenient bridge between his earlier, sometimes more personal style, and the freer, comedic sketches that were later to afford him many accolades.

Although the preceding "The District Visitor" is admittedly a funny little piece, to my mind it was " ' 'Oppy'," printed in *The Star* on December 7, 1912, that marked the beginning of Thomas' many weekly humorous short stories, published nearly every Saturday in the newspaper across three decades.

" ' 'Oppy' " is almost a quintessential Thomas yarn. The setting is a darkened London street. Our off-duty reporter wanders up to a night watchman guarding a building site. (Or is it a hole in the road? In Thomas' delightfully lopsided world, such details hardly matter.) Gaining the fellow's confidence, by means of a proffered cigarette, a friendly rapport is struck up between the newspaperman and the nocturnal guardian of this particular site. Thomas the journalist is curious to know about his station in life, and why it is that all night watchmen seem to be missing one limb. Biting off more than he can chew, our narrator then has to listen to the watchman reel off a series of conflicting and rather tall tales regarding the manner in which he lost his leg.

Silly stuff it may be, but " ' 'Oppy' " is funny, unexpected and showcases the narrative qualities and observational humour which Thomas went on to nurture and mould into his own idiosyncratic style. There is, for example, the phonetic Cockney spelling which, years later in a review of one of Thomas' books, J. B. Priestley remarked was "itself a triumph of observation." Of note also is the admirable economy of words; the writer's ability to provide a sense of "place" in the space of a few well-chosen phrases. Marry these qualities with his irrepressible sense of fun, his penchant for thinking up a ludicrous theme, and the feeling that in sketches such as this Thomas is "everyman," representing all of us, then you have, with this landmark story, a case of an author hitting upon a winning formula. The searcher after truth being talked at, not to, by the galaxy of quirky characters, from all walks of life, that he meets on his trips across London or the Sussex or Devonshire countryside.

Reading so much of his work, I've found that the perennial enigma (for me at least) with these humorous stories is how many of them were based on real life incidents, and which were the product of Thomas' fertile imagination. In most cases, I suspect the answer is a bit of both; an amalgam of everyday social observation and unashamed invention. Thomas had the storyteller's gift; the ability to spin a good yarn and know when to embellish the facts a little to make it more interesting.

But I digress. Getting back to the stories in this collection, throughout 1913 Thomas really got into his stride with regards to exploring and honing his humorous style. It is hard to pick a favourite among the articles I've included here, but for sheer laugh-out-loud brilliance, we have several contenders to the throne.

Readers will surely delight in the endearing "Poddles," which positively overflows with typical Thomasian touches. It's a vibrant sketch in which an increasingly harassed Thomas accompanies his adopted niece (actually, she adopts him!) on a day trip to Kew Gardens. His acute embarrassment at the situation he finds himself in, with the amused glances of fellow tram passengers not helping matters, is offset by his ironic, philosophical take on the proceedings. "Poddles" proves to be a very determined little girl with a one-track mind. A force of nature that he can only be swept along by as he tries to keep her under control while still maintaining his dignity.

Of equal merit is "The Quarrel," wherein Thomas pays witness to an extraordinary war of words, by means of chalk on the pavement, between two adolescent girls. But in terms of comedic spectacle, the jewel in the crown of this collection must surely be "The Stray." Its virtue lies in its well-observed and utterly ludicrous situation: the author is emotionally blackmailed by a group of opinionated onlookers who, loitering at his front gate, talk him into adopting a homeless kitten! Whether this one is based on a factual occurrence or not, with much gusto, Thomas relates this particular happening with customary verve and insight.

An altogether more personal insight into the author's life becomes apparent when one reflects that around the time these sketches were written, Thomas and his wife Louisa, recently married, had just moved into their new home in Chiswick, West London. It was in this very house, where they lived until the early 1920s, that they raised a family, having two children, Margaret and Peter. Pieces such as "The Step Maid," in which a spirited young lady offers to clean his front doorstep, and the intriguing " 'The Best People'," a reflection on local snobbery, were clearly informed by this period of Thomas' life.

Moreover, a number of the sketches in this book powerfully evoke the class divisions prevalent in this era of British history; a topic I will discuss shortly in relation to these articles.

With the invaluable assistance of my researcher friend Morgan Wallace, and with the help of the staff of Chiswick Public Library, I was able to pinpoint the exact addresses of the two houses Thomas and his family lived in during his long spell as a resident of Chiswick. In the summer of 2010, I took a trip to the area that had obviously provided the backdrop to so many of his tales of London street life. Retracing the author's footsteps, I took a long look at the largely unchanged streets of the Gunnersbury area, which Thomas commuted from across London to the offices of *The Star* for two decades (before relocating to Seaford in East Sussex at the end of the 1920s). It was an especial pleasure to stroll along the Strand-on-the-Green, a quaint and again, seemingly unspoilt pedestrian path on the north bank of the River Thames, near Kew Bridge. The beauty of this spot made it quite evident why this was one of Thomas' favourite neighbourhood walks.

Of course, these stories are almost a century old. They were penned in a vanished era, a pre-war Edwardian London that, despite what I've noted above regarding parts of Chiswick, for the most part has since changed beyond recognition. This was a world of street urchins, electric trams, and "pea soupers." A society in thrall to class distinctions, where motor-cars were driven only by the rich elite. A bygone age that the Great War was to change forever.

But despite their interest from an historical perspective, it should be noted that Thomas wrote his sketches as light entertainment. They were intended for London commuters to read on their way home by bus, train or tram, and for those reading their Saturday evening newspaper in front of the coal fire in their living room, or in the local park on a warm summer evening. They were not created to be read years later as historical documents. However, the insights, snippets of social commentary, and incidental period detail they provide us today nevertheless prove fascinating. Thomas is ever the observer, absorbing the chatter of those he meets and eavesdrops on. The humorous journalist at work who today, ironically, acts as our guide to the London of yesteryear.

Whether listening to the outpourings of housemaids, butlers, publicans, street traders, tram conductors, rag 'n' bone men, florists, or harassed mothers of unruly children, in the pieces collected in the pages of this book, he remains, for the most part, a tolerant chronicler of events. Studiously gathering material that will inspire one of his sketches, he is always able to laugh gently and good-naturedly at people's foibles.

But occasionally, and to our amusement, even in his capacity as the patient observer of everyday life, Thomas sometimes loses his rag. When this occurs, he invariably supplies the often bemused recipient of his annoyance with an erudite put-down—which is totally lost on the part of the cheeky Cockney who has pushed him that bit too far! Thus, in "The Mayflower," prior to giving Mrs. Boddy, his morose washerwoman, a good telling off, he makes the following cutting remarks about her person:

> "She is a commonplace person without an atom of poetry in her make up ... there is an ever-present sense of greyness about Mrs. Boddy."

Considering that he had recently graduated from a clerk to a journalist, and was moving upwards socially, one could be forgiven for thinking that all this sounds like snobbery on Thomas' part. However, this is distinctly unfair and out of context. For one thing his writing is, as noted above, good-natured for the most part, even if it can seem at times as if he's poking fun at the colloquialisms and vernacular of the various Cockney characters he encounters in his perambulations across the streets of London. Thomas laughs at situations, as well as indeed himself, as much as anything else.

Furthermore, to act as a counterpoint to any suspicion of social aloofness (looking down with a sneer on the working classes!), we have in this collection hilarious sketches such as "The Assault." In this piece, Thomas settles himself down in the window of a tea-shop with his muffin, hoping to sit peacefully and watch the world go by. But his planned interlude from the hustle and bustle of the capital is soon rudely interrupted by the arrival of a well-to-do lady with a highly irritating manner of speaking: "My *dear* Charlotte, it was awful.

Awful!" To add to this, Thomas is dismayed by the woman's demanding, imperious attitude to a poor young waitress who tries her best to please. "The Assault" neatly illustrates his skill in turning a teeth-grinding incident into a very funny story.

Another sketch included here that will likely raise a grin is "Domestic Repairs." With more superbly observed dialogue, anyone who has experienced the horrors of paying for the "services" of incompetent odd-job men around their house will likely smile to themselves while reading this memorable tale of woe.

Occasionally Thomas would step off the beaten track and write something quite different to his usual fare. I am particularly delighted to reprint here "The Blue Minuet," a work of studied beauty, in which Thomas lovingly describes his affection for an ornament on his mantelpiece. "The Gardener" is also written with a poetic sensibility, and was a pleasure to come across in my trawl through his stories for *The Star* in this period. Oddly moving, "The Gardener" is a bittersweet study of an old sailor's love of horticulture, and the simple spiritual pleasure he derives from nurturing his treasured roses. These two beautiful, elegant articles provide us with evidence of not only his wide thematic range, but also hint at the poetry that was to dominate much of his writing in the years to follow.

Whether commuting from the suburbs to the City, or travelling out of London to his beloved South Downs, Thomas would nearly always journey by train. (In fact, one of his grandchildren recently told me that he never did learn how to drive a car!) The scene of a jolting train carriage forms the background to a number of the sketches in this volume. And how relevant still are his meditations on the grind of the daily commute to us today! "The War of the Roses" depicts the spectacle of one-upmanship among commuters aboard Thomas' usual morning train. To his amusement, the subject of contention is how to cultivate roses. (And if this seems a recurring theme in his work, I can confirm that Thomas did indeed enjoy growing roses in his garden.)

A rather striking tale of a certain journey home from work by train across London is "The Storyteller." An inconsiderate gentleman engenders the undivided attention of his fellow passengers by narrating to his travelling companion a tall story, a tale full of unexplained hints and tantalising references. The occupants of the swaying carriage, Thomas being no exception, are dismayed when the spinner of this addictive yarn disembarks at his station before finishing the story!

In others, conceived in a similar vein to "The Assault," Thomas' enjoyment of an empty train carriage is shattered by the advent of noisy fellow passengers. "The Shepherdess" sees his previously calm train journey ruined by an old woman's running commentary on the efforts she makes to control her unruly horde of misbehaving grandchildren. Equally amusing is "The Prodigy," where once again the author pays witness to a family performance, in this instance a proud grandparent telling all within earshot how talented her baby grandson is. The joke here is that while the child is a dear little thing, Thomas observes that there is nothing particularly special about him.

One final journey worthy of a special mention is chronicled in "The Stranger." This time Thomas is travelling through central London on the top deck of a bus. Assuming that our narrator is from out of town, another passenger determines to act as an impromptu tour guide, intent on lavishing Thomas with fascinating anecdotes about the various landmarks that they pass along the way. Finding this ironic, Thomas deftly plays along with his unwanted escort.

In this collection, we can trace the transition Thomas made from the informal musings that characterised his early work for the *Morning Leader*, to the more typical observational humour for which he became better known. But it will not do to overanalyse these stories; to sacrifice them, as it were, on the altar of literary dissection. They were written with love and care, but as noted earlier on in this introduction, these sketches were composed primarily as entertainments. Bright and breezy yarns directed, for the most part, at homeward-bound workers. Little gems intended to provide a few minutes' worth of happy diversion from everyday London life and its attendant worries.

Well, here they are. Exhumed from the pages of an evening newspaper that sadly is no longer with us. I invite you to step back through the years and savour this selection of often riotously funny stories. These pieces provide glimpses of a bygone age, and it seems to me a little poignant that they date from a time that has now passed out of living memory.

There are some beautiful images here. Consider the baked potato man of "The Beacon Fire," plying his extinct trade through the gloomy streets of Edwardian London. Think of Gloria, the step-maid knocking on Thomas' front door all those years ago. Or Thomas himself on a forgotten seaside holiday, offering friendly advice and consolation to an innkeeper's daughter in "Ambition."

And remember young "Poddles," leading her adopted uncle a merry dance through Kew Gardens, tugging him along in a vain search for squirrels. One bright morning in that far off spring of 1913.

Richard Simms
Surrey, England
May, 2011

Bed and Breakfast

It wanted an hour of dusk, and the bats were flitting across and across the lane as I lifted the latch at the sign of the Priest House. A grey, unkempt dog, with chips of wood and hedge-brushings clinging to his coat, crept from beneath a bench and sniffed at my legs; and when I scratched him between the ears his stump of a tail swept a fan-shaped patch of the floor clean of its sprinkled sand. I shifted my knapsack a little (it had been very heavy those last four miles) and knocked on the bar with my ground ash. Followed the comfortable sound of carpet slippers, dragging a little along the floor, and through the curtained doorway came the landlord, blinking as one fresh from sleep.

Bed and breakfast? Well, the missus always saw to that part of the business. If I would take a seat in the parlour, he would send her in to me.

For twelve long months I had been looking forward to this: since early morning my face had been turned towards the "Priest House"; and thus far everything had happened as I had hoped, as it has happened a hundred times before, at a hundred other inns.

The parlour I had been in a score of times; the horse-hair covered furniture, the antimacassars, the case of birds, the crude coloured prints of Queen Victoria, Fred Archer, General Buller, and Tom Sayers; the shells on the mantelpiece, the photographs of Persimmon and "W. G.," and the stuffed tench caught by the landlord; all these I had known of and expected. I had met them before, at Ditchling under the Downs, at Winchelsea by the Marsh, at Piddinghoe, at Steyning, at Burpham, and Itchen Abbas.

The landlady, too, was an old friend. She would, I knew, be plump, and, as it was a Sunday evening, dressed in black silk and beads, with possibly a gold chain and locket. In two minutes the terms were fixed; bed and breakfast, three-and-sixpence; supper, one shilling; and I stooped to unlace my boots. For I was dusty and weary from my tramp, and there was a throbbing blister on my left heel.

Walk twenty miles across a dry county, away from the main roads, through the by-lanes, and over the stiles, all under a sky hazy with heat, and you will know at the end that there is no pleasure to equal the pleasure of kicking your heavy boots from your tired feet, and twiddling your toes in roomy carpet slippers.

While supper is preparing, it is good to find the red-tiled stable-yard and its green pump; to roll back your shirt, and put your head in the cooling, cleansing stream, while the landlord works the handle and hisses like an ostler.

A rough towel, and then for the cold beef, and salad fresh from the kitchen garden, the gooseberry tart and custard, the bread and cheese, and the brown stone mug with blue rings round it, the jolly pint mug, with V.R. and a crown on it as proof of its perfect honesty.

Bed and breakfast is always an adventure. Once on the Portsmouth road I shared my room with a sailor, flushed from a voyage, who awoke three times in the night to count his money, coin by coin, in a loud voice.

Then there is the adventure of the sheets, and by this standard only may an inn and its hospitality be safely judged. For if, as you sit on the garden bench with that luxurious after-dinner pipe, you see the good wife putting the clothes-horse in front of the kitchen fire, then you may be sure that the rest of your fare will be likewise good. At such inns shall you find onions of the landlady's pickling, a year in bottle, home-baked bread, and jam from last autumn's apples and blackberries.

But there are other inns, cold, half-lit, cheerless places, with no entertainment for any but the persistent drinker. They keep no round of beef in cut, they make no jam and bottle no onions; with them food for the traveller begins and ends with bread and cheese. Learning these things, the wise pedestrian will drink his drink and plod the miles to the next hostel, rather than risk a solitary evening and a hard bed, with the possibility of damp sheets.

Better to strike the road afresh, and you will surely chance on an inn where they understand, where your host will show you the last litter of puppies, where in the taproom you may listen the long evening to the sleepy drone of the farm labourers talking the gossip of the countryside, and where the sheets on your bed will be fresh with the scent of the hedgerows on which they were aired.

Your perfect innkeeper, of course, should be a jolly man, inclining to plumpness; not fat and slow to move, but cheery and rosy, with a good waist and a merry eye. He should know the countryside, who farms each field, who has a horse to sell, whose oats were blown flat last storm. In the matter of dogs and ferrets he should be the authority of his district; and his customers he should call by their first names. But above all must he know a good piece of beef.

There is an inn that I know, a sweet place, all set in roses, and the hum of bees, where I spent a night last summer, and at whose landlord I was not a little puzzled. Toward me, for the five shillings I was spending in his house, his manner was uncomfortably deferential; but to the more humbly-clad men of the soil, the men with the loam about their boots, he was cold to the verge of rudeness. With them he had nothing in common; of their lives and work he knew or cared little; and fear of his own ignorance had taught him to hold his tongue.

As I say, he puzzled me, until I noticed his mutton-chop whiskers and his manner of drawing a cork. Then I knew him for the retired butler. The inn was his hobby, not his living, and from old habit he walked quietly and judged his customers by their cloth.

So before you decide to take your bed and breakfast at the "Bladebone" or the "Winking Pedlar," do you seek out the landlord, and ask him the way to the next village. If he have mutton-chop whiskers and talk coldly, get to the road again. But if he answer you cheerily, try his fare, see if his cat be sleek and well fed, and you will stay to sleep.

And in the morning he may tell you of good fishing near by, and lend you a rod. So shall you stay for yet another night and another breakfast.

Of Saturday

The tear-off calendar which my Great-Aunt Elizabeth sent me last Christmas is beginning to look very thin and meagre, and the heat of my room has warped it almost to a semicircle. But it is fairly accurate still, and this morning it tells me that there are but 87 days left in the year, but 87 more quotations to be read and thrown into the fire.

Above those quotations is a highly coloured picture (mostly forehead) of what my Great-Aunt in her covering letter called the Swan of Avon; but if it be like Shakespeare, then Bacon unquestionably wrote the plays and poems. Certain it is that the original of my portrait could never have fathered them, and I shall take the first opportunity of putting him in the dustbin.

For that reason only I am quite looking forward to New Year's Day, when it will be obsolete, and when the Longfellow tear-off calendar, which is sure to be sent next, is going to get badly lost in the post.

The quotations are the most interesting part of the calendar, and I am just beginning to like them. It took me a long time to discover that they had any connection with the date on which they were served up; and until a week or so ago I thought the compiler had chosen them haphazard, snipping the short sentences from their setting with a somewhat irresponsible pair of scissors and very little luck.

But I misjudged him; for on September 29 I found this:

QUARTER DAY.
Angels and ministers of grace defend us!

That, I think, is decidedly a happy touch, and since that date I have been hoping to find such another, so far in vain. To-day, for instance, I read:

DIVIDENDS DUE.
Halfway down
Hangs one that gathers samphire; dreadful trade!

As a hint that one may or may not get a cheque from one's brokers on Monday, this cannot be counted a success, although I have failed to find anything more (or less) appropriate to the occasion.

To-day has never been connected in my mind with samphire. If there is anything which Saturday suggests, it is a half-day off, a morning spent clearing up the debris of the week's work, cutting off the frayed edges, and especially in listening for the clock to strike one.

Certainly it is the most genial, the friendliest day of all the week. Compared with Saturday, Monday is a miserable, a cold-blooded, callous sort of day.

Everybody seems to get up late on Monday morning, grumpy and miserable and out of tune. After the day and a half of relaxation the collar galls, the traces chafe one's sides. With Sunday morning's bad example behind you linger between the sheets until the very last minute, reducing breakfast to an irreducible minimum, and catch your train, or the one after, or the one after that, at a run, completing your journey panting and swaying between the luggage racks. And with what a cold Monday morning eye do your fellow-passengers stare disapproval at you.

Altogether it is a frightful day. Nothing goes right, the office is cold and cheerless, there is nothing before you but the week's dull round, and next Saturday seems years away.

Tuesday is a little better than Monday; one has settled down to the collar and become a little reconciled to work by Tuesday, while Wednesday is quite a joyous day. Then our straining eyes can see the week-end in the distance and work becomes almost a pleasure. Wednesday is the middle of things, the top of the hill; and hence the road drops easily to pay-day and Saturday. The hard pull is over, to-morrow is Thursday and the next day Friday. We begin to wonder about the weather, to make plans for the coming respite, to borrow shillings for lunching purposes.

So is it with Thursday, the day before pay-day, the day of adventure. The morning's post may bring invitations or acceptances of invitations. Anything may happen on Thursday to make or mar the coming interval of rest. The barometer may fall or rise, and thus decide the fate of Sunday morning. Or one may get the sack.

Of Friday only one thing need be said. It is a great getting-ready for Saturday, a talking over of plans, a making of trysts, a sending of telegrams, a paying back of loans.

There is also the cashier and his jingling envelope.

And then comes Saturday with its compartment full of smiling faces and chattering men; of girls talking about costumes and millinery and shopping; of youths with green baize bags, hockey sticks or footballs. The world gets up early and with a smile on Saturday morning. Why, in spite of this morning's fog and cold, a man I did not know actually spoke to me in the train, quite genially, too; something about the position in the Balkans. He also borrowed two matches.

That is the Saturday humour, the end-of-the-week-at-last spirit; for to-morrow there is no "last workmen's" to scamper for, no reluctant crawling from bed at the last minute or later, no abbreviated breakfast. Instead, a long, long sleep, with maybe one of those sweet disappointments when one sits up in a hurry thinking it is Monday, to sink gratefully smiling to the pillow again. That alone is worth all the days of the week.

In our youth, Saturday was a day of horror, a day of perpetual house cleaning, of disorganised meals, of extra special baths, with the corners properly done under maternal supervision, and of early bed.

If anything, Sunday was worse. Then one wore "best clothes" and stiff collars, and had to behave all day long.

Because of that, when we grow up, and can wear our best clothes (if any) all the week should we wish, we run amok through the week-end.

So this afternoon, when the clock swallows the lump in its throat and gets ready to strike one, I shall be reaching for my hat. If it be still foggy I shall go down Charing Cross-road to buy books, and if it be fine I shall go home and buy bulbs; while to-morrow I must take the dog and my pipe for a tramp along the towing-path. We are going to have a great time either way.

"This Style"

A day or two ago, urged partly by vanity, partly by a bad cold, I decided to buy me a nice woollen waistcoat; a cosy garment, neat but not gaudy; a nice warm brown with a delicate green spot here and there.

To that end I walked into an outfitter's shop and asked the price of such a waistcoat. The man behind the bar took a lot of pins out of his mouth, like a conjuring trick, pressed the palms of his hands flat upon the counter, and, taking a long breath, leaned across to me and said:

"Sem-lem, eight-lem, nine-lem, ten-lem, lem-lem."

I forbore to ask him if he could keep it up, and answered instead, "Sem-lem." And he went to get it. This by way of preface.

With his departure I stepped backward, and in so doing collided with another of the staff who had been standing close to me. "I beg your pardon!" I said; and straightaway the urchin, who was cleaning the brass plate on the door, made a lot of confused noises, and stuffed a large chamois leather into his mouth, following that up with a portion of a duster. The man into whom I had barged made no sign, so I begged his pardon again, a little more loudly.

This time it was the shop assistant, bearing my waistcoat, who made an ass of himself.

It appeared that both his bootlaces had come undone, and as he stooped to tie them I could see the veins in his neck swelling, while from inside him there came sounds as of one afflicted with the quinsy.

Then I began to understand the silence of the assaulted one. He was dumb, fashioned without speech, hearing, or sight. His flesh was of wax, his hair had once grown on a horse, his chest was hay and cardboard, his trousers were marked 10s. 6d. And oh! I did so want to smack his smug face.

The next day they had put him in the window; carried him all stiff and cold, with fixed outstretched hands and unbending knees, and posed him before a roll of Harris Tweed. Fascinated, I stopped to look at him, but he stared me out of countenance.

There was something horrible about his rigidity; his glazed eyes, one badly set, his sleek hair and immaculate moustache. I knew that inside his clothes, where should have been warm flesh and blood, there throbbed nothing but packing straw, that the legs behind the beautiful creased trousers were broom handles, that his boots contained no toes.

His perpetual smirk also annoyed me, and I became possessed with an inordinate desire to assault him. I wanted to feel my fist crunching through his miserable face, to get my hands where his heart should be and tear him asunder, to expose him for the miserable forked radish that he was.

A day later I encountered another of his tribe, aping a boy of ten, in velvet suit and Fauntleroy curls. I put my hand on his shoulder, and shuddered. It was like stroking a stuffed dog.

I hate all tailors' dummies. There is something so repellent in the confidence with which they imitate humanity. Like pillars of virtue they stand, looking neither to the right nor to the left, self-satisfied and unheeding. Motor-buses may run amok before their eyes, thrones may totter, but they go on; ever smirking, ever showing one how one really ought to dress.

That, I think, is really the secret of my hatred of them. I know quite well that I shall never have trousers like theirs for more than five minutes. They have no knees, and their garments cannot bag. My coat will never hang as do their coats, my waistcoat never be so free of wrinkles. As I look at these figures, set in the windows that we should copy them, I am reminded of a boy who went to school with me. He was a model child, both in dress and deportment, and we were often bidden to take note of his virtuous ways, and do likewise. He had never climbed a tree in all his life, had never got his hands and face dirty, never torn his clothes, was always polite to his superiors, and won hundreds of prizes. So that the rest of the school banded together to slay him, but only succeeded in daubing his lace collar and velvet blouse with clay.

That is how I feel about these lath and plaster men who wear the clothes that one day I may be reduced to wearing. I know that they are exhibited as a pattern to you and me. We are expected to cultivate these wooden legs, those broad shoulders, that tremendous chest development, that right arm forever bent to greet the dummy across the road.

So I want to smash one in the face; I want to feel my fist pushing his little pink nose out through the back of his neck; to watch him bleed sawdust and shavings.

Consider for one moment the feelings of the shop assistants: They have to dress him! They have to prop him up against a wall, and button his shirt over his empty chest. They must lay him along the counter and draw his wonderful trousers over his legs. Then there is his bow to be tied, while all the time that pink and fatuous smile stares them in the face. I admire the shop assistants, for I think they must kick him now and again.

The question of dressing these figures sets one wondering: Do they wear underclothes, vests, and the like? Is the fine white shirt a real shirt or just a "dickey" and a pair of cuffs? And if there be no shirt, is the collar nailed to the back of the neck? Do they wear braces and socks? It is an absorbing question, and one that I should like answered. Perhaps I had better buy a dummy and hold an inquest on it. Then, if it still smiled, I could jump on it.

It is the smile that is so annoying. There is a dummy woman in a Holloway shop who, during the past fortnight, has been successively a waitress, a housemaid, an actress, an ordinary woman, and yesterday, during a sale of mourning goods, she was a widow. And she smiled steadily through it all.

She would be a fitting mate for my enemy of the waistcoat shop. She looked as if she could make it hot for him, and then, of course, he would run—and I should be avenged.

Going a Journey

On Tuesday next I purpose travelling to Callowdale Magna, or as the bills of lading put it, "as near thereto as I may safely get," with due respect to such impediments as the "restraints of Rulers and Princes, Barratry, Fire, Robbery, and Jettison."

Now the road to Callowdale Magna lies along three or four of our great railways, with a short trip on a connecting loop-line. Therefore I must first travel to Chemmerstone Fourways, change there for High Potters, re-train at High Potters for Chelmer's Rise, change there once more for Mope's Causeway, and so to Callowdale Magna.

In the matter of catching trains I like above all things to have plenty of time. Knowing that a certain train leaves a certain station at 9.15 a.m., there is a tendency to dawdle on the way, thinking the while how nice it is to be able to take one's time.

Five minutes from the station it dawns upon you that you must hurry, and there follows a fierce sprint, ending with a terrific leap at the stairs, and a vision of the rear guard's van rounding the bend with, as it were, its thumb to its nose.

On that morning alone in the whole year the 9.15 a.m. is in to time, and there are no empty milk cans to be unloaded.

Therefore, having sold myself litter after litter of pups in this manner, it was my first intention to go to some big terminus where they have plenty of trains, St. Pancras or Charing Cross, and there to wait for the next to Callowdale Magna. It might be an hour or it might be two; but there are fires in the waiting-rooms at all the best stations, and there would be a book or two in my bag.

This sitting in waiting-rooms is quite good fun. Such a queer lot of people use waiting-rooms, and for such queer purposes. They come in to rearrange their clothing, to unpack their bags, to change their boots, to write letters, to adjust their complexions before the railway company's mirror, to eat sandwiches, and, in couples, to hold hands. Nobody seems to use these rooms for the purpose of waiting for trains.

As I have said, it was my original intention to wait in a waiting-room for the next train to Callowdale Magna. Then came a friend with a time-table. In five minutes he had planned it all out; how I was to take the 11.32 p.m. to Chemmerstone Fourways, arriving there at 2.2 a.m.; catch the 2.8 for High Potters, the 4.17 at High Potters for Chelmer's Rise, thence taking the 5.10 to Mope's Causeway, and so to Callowdale Magna, where I should arrive at 8.25.

He worked it all out beautifully, and I am beginning to think that it will come off. That is, if the compiler of the time-table has not been pulling my leg.

Really, you know, one has to take such a lot for granted in the matter of time-tables. For supposing the 4.17 from High Potters should not go to Chelmer's Rise at all.

I must confess that for years I mistrusted the men who make the time-tables. I thought they just put a lot of numbers into a hat, drew out a handful, doubled them, added twice the number they first thought of and so on. But my statistical friend assures me that this is wrong, and he is a bank clerk with a life-long experience of the most appalling figures.

Since he explained it all to me I no longer feel like making game of time-tables. They are subjects for reverence, and I am awed at the thought of the men who build them, men with huge crinkled foreheads.

Even now I do not profess to understand them. I am content to leave that to the men who must, the commercial travellers and the luggage porters.

Once or twice I have dived into one of these mazes, but each time have come out defeated, my head buzzing with a thousand asterisks, daggers, footnotes about restaurant cars, Saturdays only, not on Saturdays, Pullmans, first and second only, and other mysterious runes, hieroglyphics, and secret signs.

So I have learned to lean on the green-trousered porter, to look to him for light. The printed figure fails to make me comfortable where the spoken word carries conviction; and for twopence an enterprising porter will lie you into a state of absolute security; for threepence he will see that your train goes exactly when you wish.

On Tuesday next, however, I shall dispense with his help; for my banking friend has put me right. He has worked out the sum, struck a balance, and written E & O E at the bottom. So now I know it is all right.

He even went so far as to discover that by breaking my journey at Kerwick Bay and walking half a mile to Earl's Quarry, I could shorten the whole trip by about an hour. But I shall not do that. Already I have to get into five separate trains, to browbeat five lots of passengers into letting me sit down, and I have no desire to add to the number.

Getting into a fresh railway carriage is nearly as bad as walking into church in squeaking boots. There is a coldness about your reception, eyes are lifted from books and newspapers to glare and drill holes in this strange new being who thus forces his company upon an otherwise comfortable little community. You have disturbed the economy of the carriage, whose occupants, having got used to one another, have now to start all over again getting used to you.

So they grudgingly shift each a quarter of an inch, dragging their rugs and books with them reluctantly, all the time speculating on your destination, business there, and probable social standing. Once you are seated you can feel them staring at you over their papers, until the hot blushes race over your body from your feet to your hair. Then they resume their reading, and in five minutes you are accepted as part of the furniture of the compartment, are admitted into the brotherhood; and at the next stop, should another stranger enter, you will stare at him and resent his intrusion in just the same manner.

So I shall not break my journey at Kerwick Bay; but shall follow my statistician's original plan, and go straight on to Chelmer's Rise. And lest there should be any clever person ready to find a flaw in that program, I can save him a lot of trouble by pointing out that the stations mentioned above, High Potters and Callowdale Magna, Mope's Causeway, and the rest, are all of my own invention, and do not appear in any time-table. The names please me, however, and should you wish to journey to any of the villages mentioned, almost any porter at Euston or Liverpool-street will put you on the right track—for twopence.

Muffins

There are some things which the world will never take seriously; ordinary everyday things that enter the lives of all of us, such as policemen's feet, empty jam-pots, the braying of asses, the quarterns of gin, pimples, young curates, and kitchen pokers.

Now in none of these is there anything fundamentally humorous. An empty jam-pot is just an empty jam-pot, and it is nothing more. Yet we have been educated for generations into believing that an empty jam-pot is a ludicrous affair, and at any mention of it we laugh. The composer of that still popular song, "Sally broke the jam-pot," knew very well that jam-pots were humorous. Had he written "Sally broke the vegetable-dish" his song would not have lived through the ages as it has done.

Again, take the braying of asses, in itself a most melancholy sound. So sure as a coster's donkey lays his ears back, bares his teeth, and gives tongue to his desires and dislikes, nine out of ten men will stop in their walks and grin at the sight and sound of it; not one of whom would turn his head at the barking of a dog or the neighing of a horse.

Curates, too, must be young, and pimples qua pimples are not more provocative of mirth than sprained ankles. But your professional humorist has only to mention the pimple on his neck, or the pimple on the young curate, or the feet of a policeman, or a glass of gin, and straightaway his audience will roar their ribs out. He need not leer, nor make mouths, nor twist his legs one in the other, nor fall over his umbrella, nor do any of the things that are really comic. Just in his ordinary voice and manner let him say, "The young curate fell over the kitchen poker and broke his neck," and pit and gallery rock with the humour of it. It is very remarkable.

In the same category with the unfortunate feet of the policeman and the ass's bray, one must put muffins and their lesser brothers, the crumpets. They, too, have had ridicule thrust upon them, until now they are as pregnant with meaning as were the chops and tomato sauce of Bardell v. Pickwick.

Muffins stand for stuffy bed-sitting rooms in Brixton, horse-hair furniture, antimacassars, and photograph albums. Their use is coupled in the minds of the general with poorly-paid domestic servants, and the shabby gentility that runs up bills and moves at quarter day.

This quite false impression I would dispel, for to me the muffin is a poetic thing, to be counted among the quieter pleasures of life.

Muffins go with short whist and cribbage, with the games of the hearth. People who gad about know them not, and homes where they are never seen lack cosiness, quietude, and cheerfulness. You will seldom find them in the same houses as phonographs or electric stoves.

Their use is accompanied by good honest open fires, with the chimney's throat full of roaring flame. Moreover, where they are you will get good tea, and that is above rubies.

Consider also the way in which they come to you. Bread is brought to the door in a prosaic barrow by an ordinary man, and that is all. But muffins are heralded by a clangorous bell swung by the muffin-man.

See him working his Sabbath way down a suburban street, ring-ringing his bell, tintinabulating his way past half a dozen houses; then turning, warily, because of his nicely balanced load, to see if any run after him with outstretched plate. With chin well borne up he surveys the street, and if none calls, turns again and resumes his musical clamour. The muffin-man and the fire engine are the last of our travelling campanologists.

Muffins, of course, are a dainty for winter evenings, the proper accompaniment to frosts and fog. When the starlings bubble and squeak above your chimney-pots,

When icicles hang by the wall,
And Dick the shepherd blows his nail,

then it is indeed very soothing to sit on the fender, and by a great blaze in a roomful of dancing shadows, to toast the muffins for tea. The comfortable odour of them fills the house with promise of the dainties to come, so that our appetites are sharpened and our intellects awakened. Consequently the most interesting conversations take place across the tea table. At dinner one is too busy to talk until the meal is half over; but at tea time, when one does not really eat but rather dallies and flirts with the food, there is leisure for chatting.

I know of nothing better of a winter's afternoon when the lamps are lit and the world shut out, than to sit toying with tea-cup and muffin, while listening to a good talker, or failing that, reading a good book.

To have them at their best, muffins should be toasted by an expert who has served his apprenticeship by burning one or two. For there is an art in cooking the perforated dainties, just as there is in the correct brewing of tea and the making of omelettes. Not everybody can do these things.

A muffin to be a success must be held full face to a clear red fire. It must be taken away just when it is done, neither before nor after. Exactly when that moment is you must learn by bitter experience. You must spoil muffin after muffin; eat them burnt to a gritty crispness, and eat them when but half-warmed through. Thus only can you master the gentle art.

In seeking to dignify these homely but beautiful delicacies, I have been at some considerable pains to search the arts and sciences for any reference to the muffin, and I must confess to disappointment.

Of the muffin in pictorial art, I can find little or no trace; although on the sides of the sarcophagus of Amen-Hotep in the British Museum are some drawings of rude circles with little holes in them, much resembling a conventionalised muffin.

According to the Blois and Jennifer school of Egyptologists, the inscription below states that these circular objects were the cause of

Amen-Hotep's death; so the suggestion that they are intended to represent muffins falls to the ground.

In music I have been even less fortunate; there is not a trace even in the analytical program of the "Symphonie Domestique."

But at least muffins have a literature. Does not the portly Johnson use them as the fulcrum of one of his crushing arguments with Mr. Beauclerk? And did not Dickens borrow that argument, and take the Johnsonese out of it, and give it to Sam Weller? True, he changed Johnson's muffins to crumpets, but they are brothers of the kneading board, differing only in size and price:

> Next mornin' he gets up, has a fire lit, orders in three shillin's vurth o' crumpets, toasts 'em all, eats 'em all, and blows his brains out.

This in support of the principle that crumpets were wholesome.

After that, who will dare to speak disrespectfully of muffins and crumpets? If any should, you may know them for chronic dyspeptics with no digestions. For it must be admitted even by their champions that muffins are about as digestible as cold flat-irons.

"The Best People"

The neighbourhood into which I have recently moved is a very select one; the people, what are known as "the best people." That much the house agent told me; the rest I saw in my mind's eye, and up to a little while ago I tried my utmost to live up to it, to be worthy of my neighbours.

But after the terrific collapse of my futile effort to be select, I have come to the conclusion that respectability, like genius, is something that cannot be acquired. One must have it in one's blood, or one can never be counted amongst "the best people." Not the wearing of fine linen, nor the sounding of one's aitches, nor the paying of one's bills, nor the sporting of a silk hat on Sunday; none of these things of themselves can make one respectable.

The houses in the road in which I live are all of one type; they all have a side gate labelled "Tradesmen," through which one smuggles one's mutton chops and bottled beer, and firewood, and other low things. Each, too, has its front door (opening into the passage, which one calls the "hall") and through this one accepts delivery of the weekly tops of ribs, heads of celery, goods delivered by motor-vans rich with the name of some West-end firm, and such like luxuries. For these we like our neighbours to see.

On our front gates are little labels prohibiting the calling of all hawkers, men with circulars, women with art vases to exchange for discarded clothes, and seekers after old iron and bottles. Of course, we never have bottles or old clothes in our neighbourhood.

At each end of the road is an enamelled plate which warns all and sundry that "Organs and street cries are prohibited." So now you know just how select we are, and how foolish I was ever to try to live up to it all.

It was a long time before I had an opportunity of greeting my next-door neighbours, for I leave home at a disgustingly early hour in the morning, and the evenings at this time of the year are dark. Also, the fence that separates our gardens is 5ft. 6in. high.

I ultimately made the acquaintance of the lady next door in a curious manner. One Wednesday the dustman omitted to call, and by the following Friday there was no room in the dustbin for even the top of our weekly beetroot. So I put on my garden boots, and, climbing upon the piled garbage, endeavoured to tread it into a smaller compass. It was while thus raised well above the top of the garden fence that I spied the lady next door. Her sleeves were tucked above her elbows, she was very red as to the face, and in her hands she carried the domestic ashpan.

I continued my bobbing up and down, first on one foot, then on the other, then on both; jumping with clenched fists and putting in some really good work, until the lady over the fence glanced up and caught my eye.

It was rather an awkward moment, so to help matters I said "Good morning," still bobbing up and down in the dustbin. She made no sign, so "Good morning," I said again, a little more loudly, and at that she popped indoors like a weasel.

I suppose no really respectable person would greet a lady while he was dancing in a dustbin; but how does one find out these things? I only wanted to be neighbourly; and there is nothing in the "Rules of Polite Society, by a Member of the Aristocracy," which I have since acquired, that seems to cover the situation.

However, a day or two after this, I met the lady in the street, all black beads and perspiration, and bowed to her. Afraid, probably, that if she cut me I should publish it abroad that she emptied her own ashpan, she bowed in return, and I was now an accepted acquaintance of Mrs. Wellington-Boote (I learned her name from a wrongly-delivered pound of sultanas).

Our acquaintance prospered, and from nodding, Mrs. Wellington-Boote and her husband began in a month or so to smile stiffly at me.

Once they called, but I was "out," peeping through the curtains upstairs.

So things went on for a long time, our relations growing more intimate, until I began at last to feel myself not only in the neighbourhood, but of it. I was introduced by Mr. Wellington-Boote to his daughters, to a man on the Stock Exchange, to a sidesman, to a lot of people like that, and as I came to know yet more of them I felt myself growing more and more respectable and select. Until one fatal day, when I came down with a rush, and won my freedom.

Now, if I like I can go out without a collar, for Mrs. Wellington-Boote knows me not.

I was taking Helen and Billy, my niece and nephew, out for a walk, and at the top of the hill it struck us that it was just the sort of day on which one should run and scream. (You must have felt like that yourself.)

Well, we ran down the hill, and we screamed like Red Indians, and Helen won, and I was fast gaining on Billy, who was shrieking, "Go it, Fatty!" when round the corner came Mrs. Wellington-Boote. I spun my right arm like the sail of a windmill, and thus managed to swerve enough to miss her, but I forgot to turn off the yell. So I tore past my stately neighbour, bellowing "Ululululu!" in the manner of the Somalis at the Crystal Palace. This in a road where organs and street cries are prohibited.

And now we do not speak. The sidesman, too, is noticeably colder, and reads his newspaper when he sees me coming.

But I am free, and if I wanted to do so, could walk down the street in my carpet slippers with a beer jug in each hand. I sing ribald songs as I dig in the garden, and go out on the Sabbath in a soft hat, and yell across the road to the milkman, and argue on the doorstep with the rate-collector, and do all the things that are not done by "the best people."

For these folk were ready to accept me, knowing nothing of me, because I behaved myself with decorum in the street. Respectability was the value they put on my clothes, and, for all they cared, I might have been a burglar in my spare time or run my drawing-room as a faro den. But so long as I walked sedately in the same straight line, wore a hard hat, washed my face, and did not whistle in the street I was a fit acquaintance for Mr. and Mrs. Wellington-Boote and all the younger Wellington-Bootes; and now, because I chose to be carried away by a spring morning in November, I am a social outcast, and well satisfied so to be.

But I am afraid that before long Mrs. Wellington-Boote will be goaded into asking me to move, and I do not want that; so for her peace of mind I should like to assure her that the facts concerning our dustbin-ashpan meeting are quite safe with me.

The "Wow-Wow"

For months I have studied this animal, have tracked him to his secret places, watched him at his play, and spied upon him in his feeding-grounds. And now I want to issue a Warning, to sound the tocsin and the timbrel, to rouse public opinion against him. For he is a Danger. Tracts should be written against him, societies formed for his obliteration, and he should be Put Down before he spreads.

In vain have I searched the many treatises on teratology for any mention of the breed, and Buffon and the "Lancet" are alike silent. Nor can I find word of him in "Sartor Resartus."

But by these marks you shall know him.

He wears a green hat of the Homburg variety, with its bow at the back, and its brim turned down all round. Not bent merely at the front or the back, or at either side, but sloping downwards on all sides, hiding his hair and his eyes and his ears; like an oval pent-house or a perambulating marquee. His socks are made from the designs of a tenth-rate scene painter, and executed by a drunken Cubist. And he says, "Wow-wow."

On every possible occasion he says it; in sleeping, in waking, in eating, in drinking, in working, in playing, in walking, in riding; everywhere and everywhen he says "Wow-wow," always. And although I have so far had no opportunity of verifying this, I quite expect he says it in his bath.

"Wow-wow," he says, the beast!

As a rule, he is young, maturing in the seventeenth year, and undergoing a metamorphosis after about a decade. And all the time he says "Wow-wow." It is his battle-cry, his slogan, his greeting, his farewell, his purr, his bark, his love-song, and the note of his rage.

I have found him most at street corners in the suburbs, where in groups of three or four he pretends to lean upon a fragile cane, saying "Wow-wow" at intervals, with his repulsive green hat turned down all round—a loathsome sight. Further, that the public may see his socks, he turns his trouser legs up and up and up, until his knees are almost bare. And never by any chance does he fasten the bottom button of his waistcoat.

Yet by none of these outward and visible signs may you know him from other and similar pests. Not until you have actually heard him give tongue can you be certain that you have lighted upon the true Wow-wow; and his manner of doing this varies with the occasion.

First there is the Wow-wow Courteous. Three Green Hats will be at their favourite pastime of pretending to lean upon their canes at a street corner, when a fourth Green Hat is seen approaching. As he passes the group they peer from beneath their everlastingly-turned-down-all-round hat brims, and should the newcomer be attached to their particular herd, all three will say "Wow-wow, Bertie." Pat comes the answer to the salutation, "Wow-wow, you chaps."

Next you must listen for the Wow-wow Valedictory. For a whole evening, maybe, a little knot of Green Hats has stood at a street corner under a lamp, smacking their shoe-tips with their canes in the intervals of pretending to lean upon them, and saying, "Wow-wow" steadily one to the other. At last the pack breaks up, and at parting, says each to each and all, "Wow-wow, Reggie. Same time to-morrow!" And so sure as to-morrow dawns and darkens to night, you will find them under the lamp again, saying "Wow-wow."

One fine afternoon about a month ago I came across two beautiful specimens in a tube-train, and by getting near to them unobserved, was able to study several different varieties of their tribal remark, including the Wow-wow Congratulatory, the Wow-wow Appreciative, and the Wow-wow Derisive. Had I been alone with them, and armed with a club, I should certainly have collected them.

They had taken advantage of the fact that they were seated to pull their trouser legs still higher, until those garments became almost useless; and not being able to lean upon their sticks, they twiddled them unceasingly between finger and thumb. Said the first Green Hat,

"Saw Dora last night, Willie. She'd been to a whist drive. Looked awfully dossy. Think she's a bit sweet on me." Said Willie, "Wow-wow!" (and I very nearly broke a good tooth). That was the Wow-wow Congratulatory. There was a note of envy in it, a "lucky dog" atmosphere about the way it was purred, that picked it out from the ruck of Wow-wows.

Presently there entered the train a lady, and as she swept past, the two Green Hats were tipped a little backwards, while the eyes beneath them looked up and down the newcomer as one looks over a horse. "Wow-wow!" they said to each other, quietly. True, they allowed the object of their admiration to get out of earshot before they spoke, but in the tone of their exclamation was a suggestion of the smacking of lips. That was the Wow-wow Appreciative.

But how I longed to have those two Green-Hatted insects pinned to a cork, writhing, uncomforted by camphor.

The third example, the Wow-wow derisive, was directed at me. In leaving the train I had to pass the four prismatic socks, and in endeavouring to dodge them I kicked one; whereupon I advised its owner to fold himself up a little, to retrieve his outlying parts, and to have some consideration for other folk.

He let me get out of the train, he let the door be closed, he let the train begin to move; and then, through the glass of the window, I saw his sneering lips saying "Wow-wow."

To-day I chanced upon a slightly less objectionable variety. He was standing on the steps of a club in Piccadilly, and he did not wear the regulation Green Hat. But his glossy topper was well down over the nape of his neck, and his spats looked like an accessory to some Oriental game of chance. Another man approached and passed up the steps, raising his right hand in greeting to the first. "Wow-wow," said the exquisite. But somehow it was different to the suburban variety. There was culture in the accent, and one noticed the Oxford "lilt." The vowel sounds, too, were fuller and rounder, and obviously came from a good chest.

I waited near by in the hope of hearing it again, but while disappointed of that, I saw something that was alone worth my trouble.

I saw my friend of the spats complete his toilet by inserting a monocle in his eye.

First he breathed on it, and delicately cleaned it with his kerchief. Then he took it between the finger and thumb of his right hand, and slowly opened his mouth. At the first screw, the piece of glass would not fit between his eyebrow and his cheekbone. So he opened his mouth still wider, and his chin went down and his eyebrows went up until I began to think he would never get his jaws together again. At last a stupendous yawn came to his assistance, and the monocle went home. Then I found that my own mouth was open. I had been helping him with my moral support, and had forgotten to close it.

But about these Green-Hatted Wow-wows who play the Bohemian and the gay dog and the nut under the village lamp-post at Turnham Green and Upper Holloway and Tooting. I want a League, a Society, an Association, or a Law. I want their close season abolished. I want their blood, and if somebody does not do something, one of these nights I shall club one to death.

And when the judge puts on the black cap, and asks me if I know of any reason why sentence should not be passed upon me, I shall say "Wow-wow," and walk to the scaffold with a springy step.

The District Visitor

I was carefully rounding the point of my left jaw, that tricky corner where all the accidents happen, when the bell downstairs rang and the knocker rapped out five shorts and a long. Through the lather on my face a faint pink flush grew and darkened to rose, and a little sanguine tear trickled to the point of my chin … The bell and the knocker were again simultaneously agitated.

Now, I devoutly thank whatever gods there be that I have no friends who both knock and ring. Some do the one, some do the other—some, again, do neither; but no one does both. When Billy comes, for instance, he just yells "Fatty!" through the letter-box, while his disreputable little sister climbs the back gate into the garden, to the scandal of the neighbourhood and the mutilation of her stockings. Therefore I was curious about this visitor whose double-barrelled alarum had caused me to cut myself.

People who use both knocker and bell may be known at once for superior folk. There is something peremptory about their double summons that picks them out from the ruck of humanity and its simple dropping of the knocker. Though there be no "Knock and Ring" plate on your door to guide them, faced with a knocker and a bell they know exactly what to do. Brought up from birth as they are in an atmosphere of bells and knockers, their ambidextrous doorstep duet has a verve about it which one finds only with the cultured. Knocking and ringing begin together and end together. There is no overlapping, no ragged ends; the last pulsation of the bell's clapper synchronises perfectly with the final descent of the knocker.

This is by no means as easy as may at first sight appear. Try it for yourself. Try to push the china button with your left hand while performing a well-timed "pom-tiddley-om-pom—pom-pom" with your right.

Like grace in the consumption of asparagus or dignity in the admonition of fraudulent cabmen, it is a gift; and by no amount of study can you acquire it.

All this long time I am hurriedly scraping the other side of my face, while from below at intervals comes that urgent twofold summons. In a few seconds the shave was complete, the blood mopped up, and I scrambled into a nice clean collar. But by the time I had got down to the door the aristocratic unknown had gone, leaving not a wrack behind but a yellow pamphlet sticking through the letter-box. So I went upstairs again, took off my nice clean collar, and put on something comfortable.

The booklet was the parish magazine issued from the Vicarage of St. Alphege-under-the-Willow, price twopence; and inside was a card which said "Mrs. Jermyn Paton," and in the corner "2nd Tuesday."

Two days later she called for the twopence, and as I did not wish her to make a practice of coming I asked her inside.

She was a large, rustling, well-preserved lady, dressed for the most part in dead animals. There were stoats and weasels on her head, and foxes and wolves round her neck, and minks and skunks and squirrels and badgers hanging all over the rest of her. And everywhere I looked I saw little furry heads with staring glass eyes and tiny pink tongues, dangling around her like scalps on a Red Indian. Some such fashion exists, I have read, among the Igorottes and the Anthropophagi, and such untutored folk to whom we send tracts and missionaries.

I had not been talking to her for ten minutes before I saw quite clearly that the planning and creation of the lower animals had been ordained and carried out only that Mrs. Jermyn Paton might not feel the cold.

She did not take long to get to business. Had I taken the whole house? Rarely! Did I like the neighbourhood? Rarely! Not at business to-day? Oh, rarely! Did my business at home? No, rarely? Er—what was my business? Rarely! Did I attend St. Alphege? Oh, rarely? But surely my house was in her parish? Was that so, rarely? The boundary ran through the garden? Right through a Canterbury bell? Not rarely? But boundaries did not really matter, and the vicah, the Reverend Mr. Challice, was such a delightful man and such a parful preacher; quite broad and up-to-date in his views. "In fact," said this Person, "I am sometimes given to wondering if he rarely does not go too far." She wished I would come and hear him one evening. She was sure I should be so delighted, rarely!

Here I thought it incumbent on me to make my position plain. In matters religious, I said, my convictions were entirely my own, and a dead secret. Politically I was an Anarchist (nor rarely?), with a drawer full of red ties in my bedroom; and I always wore flannel next to my skin. My worst vices were reading in bed and warm burgundy; my only virtue a love of dogs. Then, lest she should forget to ask, I told her my income (or what I thought it ought to be), the story of my parentage and upbringing (very harrowing this), the reason the grandfather clock in the hall did not go, the number of rooms in the house, and how many were really furnished, and what we paid a pound for tops of ribs.

I gave her the most interesting and inaccurate details of my private life, I cut the traces of my imagination and let it bolt. But it was all of no use. She did not turn a hair, but sat rigid on the ultimate edge of my chair, and lapped it all in as bull-pups lap milk.

To my every statement she drawled her everlasting "Rarely!"; now as a note of interrogation, now as an expression of surprise, or doubt, or fear, or indignation. Had I said I had just killed and eaten all my grandparents, I feel sure she would have dragged out a "Rarely!" though she might have edged a little nearer the door.

Continuing the horrid tale, I pointed out that I had not had time to look at her magazine (Rarely!), and not feeling interested, did not propose to pay the twopence. But I was quite ready to toss her fourpence or nothing for it.

At this, all the little furry corpses on her ample person trembled with righteous indignation, and she rose to go.

She did not quite understand me, she said. The magazine had been in my possession for two days, and I ought, in common decency, to pay for it. It was not a question of twopence more or less, but a matter of local patriotism. "Not rarely," I said.

And so she went, probably to report me to the vicah. But she has not been since, which is exactly what I wanted; and I am looking for a little enamelled plate for the front gate, with the legend, "No Hawkers, No Bottles, No District Visitors."

" 'Oppy"

From my youth up this thing had been worrying me. A hundred times I had asked myself the question: Why must a man be maimed for life before he can be a night watchman? Was there ever a night watchman who had two complete legs and two complete arms? Was there ever an absolutely unabridged night watchman with two eyes, ten fingers, and ten toes?

To the unthinking person it may appear that I was worrying myself unnecessarily, that a man can night watch as well with one arm as with two.

Sitting in his little sentry-box, surrounded by red lanterns, and warmed by a cheery coke fire in a perforated pail, your night watchman may look an insignificant enough person. But consider his responsibilities! During the day an army of workmen has been spreading macadam, or digging holes, or building houses. With dusk the day's work ceases, and our friend takes up the tale. All through the long and dreary nights he will guard those houses, those holes, that macadam. And when morning dawns and his fire has paled to grey ash, you will find him at his post, houses, holes, and macadam intact, and the steam roller where you left it overnight.

From sunset to sunrise you may see him, now tottering round from lantern to lantern, tending his wicks, now on the look-out with his night glass to his eye (or is it a beer can?).

Does it not strike you as somewhat absurd that the men upon whom all this responsibility devolves should have to be mutilated in some way before they can obtain employment? Why, they never know when they may be called upon to defend a stack of scaffold poles, a water-cart, or a tar-boiler. And of what use in such an emergency is a man with but one arm or leg?

From my early days, when I used to put water in the oil-can from which he filled his lamps, I have had a growing respect for the night watchman. Whenever I see a coke fire and a sentry-box I try to get a peep at the custodian, to see what portion of him has been chipped off, and only once have I found an unimpaired specimen. He was a nonagenarian, and was minding Old Broad Street.

But always have I looked upon them as pillars of honesty, men of unswerving integrity. Old soldiers, broken in their country's wars, I told myself; neglected by an ungrateful public for whom they had sacrificed their limbs at a shilling a day.

True, I had had no chance of verifying this melancholy picture until a day or two ago, when a small army of men pitched their camp just opposite my front door, and commenced to dig a large hole.

At nightfall came the watchman up the street, pitter-bump, patter-bump, complete with wooden leg and perforated pail. I watched him light his lanterns, and listened as he apostrophised the breeze. When his fire was crackling merrily I went out to interview him on the subject that had been so long engrossing me.

He was sitting in his box when I arrived, and by way of opening the conversation I spread my hands over his glowing coke, and coughed a little.

"If you young beggars don't git out of it—" he began; then leaned from his hut, saw me, and said, "Oh, it's you!"

"Excuse me, Mister Watchman," I said.

"My name's 'Oppy," he answered; "always was and always will be. Wodjer want?"

I took some coppers out of one pocket and put them ostentatiously into another.

"Just dropped in for a chat," I said. "Thought you might feel lonely, you know."

"Gotter fag?" was his only comment, and, his need being supplied, I proceeded.

"Been on this job long?" I asked.

"Forty-one year," he said. Then musingly, "It's 42 year come Candlemas that I lost me leg. Fell off a stepladder takin' down Christmas 'olly and mistletoe, and I got the job in the following year. Down at Lime'us that was, where I lodged with my married sister. Forty-two year come Candlemas, and since then I've minded 'ouses and chapels and churches. Yes, and cathedrals I've minded. And never lost one neither. Forty-two year come Candlemas.

"It was in '72 I lost me leg, or was it in '71? Any 'ow, I was mate on a Shields schooner at the time, and fell off the main truck in a gale off Havver in France. Broke me leg, went to 'orspital, surgeon drunk, set it wrong, 'ad to 'ave it off. Forty-two year come Candlemas." He sighed deeply, and stirred his fire with his iron-shod stump.

"I minded a Town 'All once, up at Nottingham. 'Taint everybody as can mind Town 'Alls. As a rule they only take old soldiers, but they made an exception with me, seeing as 'ow I'd lost me leg.

"Yes, my cousin 'Enery was on the same boat when I done it. A Barque out of Melbourne she was, and we was a bathin' one 'ot day round some of them there coral islands. I 'ears 'Enery 'ollerin' to me, and I looks round and sees a little black three-cornered thing a scootin' through the water like billy-o! Course, I knew it was a shark, and I put it all out, I can tell you. But it weren't no use. 'E got my leg. Clean's a whistle—scrunch! Forty-one years come Candlemas, or was it forty-two? … Scrunch! Gotter fag?

"You 'ave to 'ave a good discharge sheet before you can get a job night-watchin'. They don't let any sort of a man 'ave the lookin' after of their steam rollers, an' water-carts. You gotter be temprit an' plucky, too. Don't suppose I should 'ave got this job if our Old Man 'adn't been in the Territorials. You see, 'e knew about the Bore War, an' Paddyberg, an' 'ow I lost me leg gettin' the guns off. Forty-one years come Candlemas."

Here it began to dawn upon me that 'Oppy was pulling my leg, respecting the loss of his own. So I remonstrated with him.

"Mr. 'Oppy," I said, "you have had two of my cigarettes, but I cannot say that you have treated me at all fairly in return."

"Wodjer mean?" he asked.

50

"Well, maybe the mistake is mine," I explained, "but since I came here you have described the manner in which you lost four of your legs, and you still have one left. Did you start life as a centipede, Mr. 'Oppy? Did you not lose some legs at Waterloo and Sebastopol and Majuba?"

"Now, look 'ere, guv'nor," said 'Oppy, "anybody can see as you're wide-oh. The straight-ology of it is this 'ere. I used to be a copper, on the Tower Bridge; and one day as the bridge was a-comin' down, I got me leg in the openin', where it shuts up— Oh, well! Let bygones be bygones, guv'nor ... 'Ave you got a garden? Well, 'ow about a couple of nice two-foot earthen drain-pipe lengths? Look all right, one each corner of the lawn, with a shrub in 'em. I can drop 'em over the back-gate to-night, and a tanner won't bust you."

And this, thought I, is the man they allow to mind banks and cathedrals and water-carts; this is my sturdy sentinel, my model of integrity. Thinking which I went home, double-bolted the front door, put the chain on, and looked to my window fastenings. But I should like to know the real truth about 'Oppy's leg.

The Step Maid

Once upon a time my letter-box was but a horizontal slit in the front door, with an iron flap outside. On that flap was the word "Letters," lest any misguided person should endeavour to deliver the washing or the leg of pork through it.

Discovering that Binkle, alleged by the man from whom I bought him to be an Irish terrier, had eaten a postal order, a letter from aunt, and a demand note for the Inhabited House Tax, I decided to have a box built over the aperture; and there it stands unto this day to witness if I lie.

It was before the box was built that I first met Gloria, and this was the way of it. When the bell rang I was not dressed for company; my toilet, here and there, was incomplete. So I tip-toed to the front door, and with a penknife gently lifted the flap of the letter-box and peeped through.

Framed in the slit I saw two eyes and a piece of a nose. Gloria was peeping, too, from the other side.

What lay above and below those eyes I had no means of knowing. They were pretty eyes, grey, with long lashes, and I imagine a mouth to match, full and ripe and red. She would be about five feet six, thought I, with a lot of chestnut hair pencilled with gold; and I wished I were more completely dressed. While I was thinking all this, I had of course dropped the flap. The position was too embarrassing, and I heard Gloria giggle.

Before I could make up my mind as to the correct course of procedure, the flap rose again, and the little finger that pushed it brought the fair maiden of my fancy tumbling headlong to earth. It was so blue with cold, and so grimy. Then through the slit in the door her breath came frostily in clouds, and "Ken I clean yer step, guv'nor?" she asked.

In our suburb, you must know, everything depends upon one's doorstep. Let it be habitually soiled, and you will never be received among the elect, never be asked to whist drives in the parish room, never be accepted by the people who go to the local Empire in evening dress. With an electric bell and a tradesman's entrance, one has a position to keep up.

All this had worried me for a long time. That narrow sill of stone I knew must rival the lily for purity during at least ten minutes of the day. How soon it became dirty again did not matter. The point is that one must have one's step cleaned, and by some outside agent. Clean it yourself, with the vicar calling one never knows when, and you become a social outcast, a pariah.

Therefore one employs a step girl; such as was now breathing heavily through my letter-box.

"Ken I clean yer doorstep, guv'nor?" she asked.

I stooped to the letter-box and said, "If you will wait a few moments I'll open the door." By the time she had whistled "Alexander's Rag Time Band" twice through, with wonderful precision and perfect pedal accompaniment, I was downstairs again. She came in and stood on the mat, putting a twist of her drab hair into her mouth and rubbing her boots nervously together.

"And where might your pail be?" I asked.

"Kiddin', ain't yer?" she replied. "Why, it's your pail and your flannel and your 'arthstone of course, silly."

In an effort at being severely parental, I asked if that was how they taught her to speak at school.

"Oh, school!" said she; "we got a 'oliday," and then primmed up her mouth to a little red bud. "If you'd laike me to speak as I am taught at school, I can do so," she said; and tone and accent were perfect.

"No, I think the other suits you better," I said brutally; "get the pail and flannel."

The step was cleaned in record time, to the tune of the "Galloping Major," and in response to the rattling of the letter-box flap I went to retrieve my pail.

"Ken I come twice a week?" asked the girl as she wiped her poor red hands on her "tammy." I gave her a standing order to that effect.

"And now what is your name?" I asked.

"Glawyer," she replied; "what's yours?"

I know it looks all wrong, as if I had made that up. I did not believe it myself at first. Her tousled hair, her pink flannel petticoat, with its fringe hanging in loops, the tape garter encircling her boot; these said that her name should have been Poll or Ann or Liz, something monosyllabic and lowly.

"Trufe an' honour, guv'nor; see that wet, see that dry, it's Glawyer." She drew her forefinger slowly across her throat and made a gurgling noise, seeing which I believed.

"Well, Gloria," said that little person's new employer, "and what do people pay you for cleaning a step, pail, water, flannel, and hearthstone provided? Do you clean many in this road?"

"Number free an' four an' eight an' 'leven," said Gloria. "Number 'leven gives me tuppence, an' number free gives me a penny, an' number—well, they mostly gives me a penny, but number 'leven gives me tuppence."

It was 33 Fahrenheit in both sun and shade, and the water was bitter, and her fingers were cracking with cold, and they gave her a penny mostly; all except the kind soul at number eleven. She made it tuppence. Ignorance on her part, no doubt. And the people at number four have a girl to take their baby out. I suppose they pay her a penny, too, and if she doesn't get the baby killed or stolen, maybe they give her an old blouse at the end of the year.

"Gloria," I said, "when you go to your other customers again, tell them that you've got a new one. Tell them that at number nine you get fourpence—no, bust 'em, tell 'em you get sixpence, and an apple, and a piece of cake, and—and—and a pair of stockings. Tell 'em any old thing you like. Tell 'em—"

Gloria cut in, "Don't you worry, mate, I can make up a few on my own 'ook, I can. I'll learn 'em."

I gave her the apple, and the cake, and held out the sixpence. She backed and went pink. "Straight?" she asked; then, "Lummy, I won't 'arf tell 'em the tale neither. Leave it to me, old sport. So long—Heverybody's doin' it, doin' it, doin' it."

I knew my reputation as a man of wealth and generosity was safe in Gloria's keeping, and evidently she had the good sense not to overdo it. At number three she got a rise of twopence the following week, and number eight added a penny to their dole.

Two days ago as I was closing the door behind Gloria, she turned and held out a little packet. "Somethink for yer," she said, and bolted. Inside the crumpled piece of newspaper was a cigar, a little frayed, and a sheet from an L.C.C. exercise book. On this last was written in a fine full hand, down-strokes thick, and up-strokes thin, "In Affectionate Remembrance."

The Legacy

If this should meet the eye of Mr. Gibson Holliday, I should like him to understand that I have had just about enough of him. He palled two months ago, then he bored me, now he annoys me, and very soon he will infuriate me. Everywhere I go, everything I do, say, borrow, or buy, I run my head against Mr. Gibson Holliday and his funny little ways.

When I moved into No. 5 ("the 'ouse with the bloomin' mad blood-'ounds" the milk boy calls it, meaning Binkle, whose milk teeth are just dropping out, and who thinks it proper to treat all callers as tramps until advised to the contrary) the agent, in a reverential whisper, said, "Mr. Gibson Holliday was our last tenant." And as he said it methought he sighed, as who would say, "Ah, me! When comes such another?"

For two or three weeks I busied myself in marking Mr. Holliday's correspondence, "Not known," or "Gone, left no address," and handing it back to the postman. I also sent away one good oaken bookcase, a deed which I hope may count for something one of these days; because my books stand in piles in the corner of my room, and when I want Browning or Bradshaw or the A.B.C., there is a tremendous avalanche of literature burying me to the knees.

Two days later I found a man in the front garden with a pair of shears, giving the golden veronica a haircut. "Mr. 'Olliday's orders," he assured me. I pointed out that no doubt Mr. Holliday would also pay if he could be found, but that he had moved, and I had no intention— That is why one end of the golden veronica is three inches higher than the other.

I also refused a pair of newly soled and heeled boots (the temptation was really great, but the boots were too small!) and a copy of the Parish Magazine. Then one evening I found a lad in my garden dumping a barrow-load of mould over the graveyard of my daffodil bulbs. He had always come in that way, he said, by climbing the back gate and unbolting it from the inside. The mould was for Mr. 'Olliday. He always had it in December for his roses.

There must be a huge profit on garden mould, for when I pointed out the mistake to the lad's proprietor, he said I could have it free if I liked to keep it. And that is all I have ever got out of Mr. Gibson Holliday, except a little fun and a deal of annoyance.

Apart from the carelessness of the man in ordering bookcases to be sent to No. 5 when he must have known he was moving, there is the fact that Mr. Holliday was a man with a kind heart. So I spend my days turning from my door people who think I ought to have a kind heart, too. They come for the "half-crown you so kindly contributed last year, Mr. Holliday"; boot-club treasurers, beanfeast promoters, and people whose one object in life is the putting down of something or the promoting of the same thing.

If and when I move again I shall make judicious inquiries in the neighbourhood, and unless my predecessor was a crusty old curmudgeon I shall not take the house.

At ten o'clock of a bitterly cold night last week there came to my door three little girls—Isabel, Jessie, and Maud—and as the gas in the hall danced in the draught I asked them in on the mat.

Said Isabel, "Please, Mister Rolliday, can you give us three tickets, please, Mister Rolliday?"

"For the tea in the Iron Room, please, Mister Rolliday," said Jessie.

"Same's larsh year," said Maud.

They stood in a row, their red fists withdrawn into the sleeves of their jackets, their boots rubbing one against the other nervously.

"They're my cousins, please, Mister Rolliday," said Isabel presently, and drew a long breath.

"We're her cousins," said Jessie and Maud.

I did not know what to do or say, and my silence was scaring them.

"We've bin every Sunday when our boots was all right," continued Isabel, and her eyes were big like a cow's, with fright or expectancy.

"I'm very sorry," I said, "but Mr. Holliday does not live here now, and I haven't his new address." Their little heads dropped an inch or two, and they moved slowly towards the door. Jessie, I think, was wiping her cheeks on the corner of her pinny.

"But wait a minute," I said, for I saw a chance of learning something about this beastly skeleton in my house. "Who is Mr. Holliday? What is he like? What does he do?"

"I thought you wasn't 'im at first," said Isabel, " 'cos 'e 'ad whiskers, but I thought I'd ask in case."

From Isabel's evidence it appears that Mr. Holliday is an elderly gentleman with whiskers "the shape of King George's," and he gives teas, and brake rides, and buns, and lemonade to the regular attendants at a certain Sunday school. "An' 'e imitates a man sore-in' wood with 'is mouth, at our treats," said Maud. But he had gone, and none knew where. Their teacher didn't know, and they expected there wouldn't be no more treats. And one of them was crying on my doormat, so I told them to call again the next evening and I would see what I could do.

We had a merry little tea-party of five, for Jessie brought with her a little brother, one Ronald. " 'E don't go to Sunday school, Mister Rolliday, do yer, Ronnie? But if I didn't bring 'im I couldn't come, could I, Ronnie? 'Cos I've got to mind 'im, ain't I, Ronnie?"

Isabel watered the tea to the correct tint, and wasn't she a proud kiddie when I told her to pour out! After tea the boy wanted to know if I kept a gramophone. I did not, but there was a piano, and Isabel showed me how to play "Who were you with last night?" one finger. During the evening the neighbours had further evidence of the cosmopolitan nature of my musical repertoire, but I did not give an imitation of a man sawing wood with his mouth.

Just before they went Ronald had an accident, in which a glass of lemonade, some blancmange, and a hearthrug were concerned, whereupon Jessie told him that if he didn't behave she shouldn't bring him again. So you see what Mr. Gibson Holliday has let me in for.

The whole show, including the slight damage to the hearthrug, could not have cost more than three shillings; but somehow I am afraid I have not heard the last of Mr. Holliday's tea fights. Therefore, I am anxious to get into touch with him. I think he should have circulated a notice of his removal among his clients, and not have left poor me to carry on the business.

I am beginning to lie awake at nights, worrying about it, and already I have contracted the habit of peeping through the letter-box before I open the door. My pulse jumps at every knock, and I am hourly expecting more children. At any moment the entire Sunday school may drop in, and if they all cry on my doormat—!

Domestic Repairs

One of the familiar sights in our suburb on a Saturday afternoon is the procession of the timber-bearers; silk-hatted City men carrying great chunks of wood, strips of deal, or long poles. I see them every fine week-end, manoeuvring their burdens gingerly, and making a big circuit at the dangerous corners.

Later, the solemn quiet of my garden is chequered by the tapping of innumerable hammers, the hoarse coughing of many saws, and loud cries for somebody to hold the ladder.

Instead of being annoyed at all this, I merely become possessed of a great envy at the sound of those hammers. It tells me of men busily building pergolas and chicken-houses against the spring. On Friday they buy baulks of timber and nails and things, and on Saturday they carry them home, and there spring into being beneath their nimble fingers countless cold frames, and meat-safes, and dovecotes, and greenhouses.

But I, alas! have no power over a hammer, a plane is as useful to me as a sextant, and I wield a saw with the same dexterity with which I darn socks.

Whenever I want a greenhouse I have to buy one ready made, and my forcing frames I get from the grocer at fourpence each.

Wood and nails and hammer and saw in my hands do exactly as they wish; the wood splits, the nails bend, the hammer goes berserk, and every saw I have ever pushed had a crooked blade that simply made a jagged wound in the timber.

Only last September one of my dahlias fell before a gale or a cat, and it became necessary to fit it with a splint. One slack afternoon I fashioned a nice stick, pointed the end (and ruined a table knife), drove it into the soil beside the plant, and lashed the two together.

I was proud of that, and walked up and down the garden to see the effect of my work from different points of view. It was a good stick, solid and upright, and built to resist the gigantic storm-wind of the equinox.

Later, at the inquest on the dahlia, Mr. Perryman, who really grows the flowers that I brag about, pointed out that the stick had been driven through two of the flower's most vital underground organs.

"Confound that boy," said I to Mr. Perryman, "I'll put the sticks in myself in future. He shan't touch the garden any more."

That was my last effort, and shortly afterwards I discovered 'Erb. On his door-plate he says "Windows Cleaned by Contract. Domestic Repairs Executed."

If you see that door-plate, hurry past; for 'Erb is a mucker, a wrecker of homes. Listen!

A month ago I bought a plate-rack, and the night being dark, carried it home. For a fortnight it stood upon the floor waiting to be fixed, and on my free evenings I would wander into the scullery and look at it sorrowfully.

I had tried many times to drive nails into pink plaster. There seems to be a knack in it.

Then 'Erb came. "Easy, dead easy!" he said, and went home for his tool-bag.

On his return he was accompanied by a lad of 14, known as 'Erry. 'Erb and 'Erry. Comedy Duo and Knockabouts.

They removed their coats and waistcoats, and 'Erb did something with a collapsible ruler.

With occasional side glances at the plate-rack as if he would measure its powers of resistance, 'Erb mounted a chair and stepped into the sink.

Damping his right palm with his tongue, he desired 'Erry to hand him the hammer. At the very first blow 'Erb struck the nail squarely on the head, and some plaster fell into the sink, about a pound.

Nothing discouraged, he tried again lower down. He tried all over the wall, so that the sink was full of plaster. He drove nails everywhere, until the plate-rack looked like a porcupine.

Then he turned to 'Erry and said, "What we want for this 'ere job is annover 'ammer and some putty." So 'Erry went to get them, while 'Erb wiped his face on my towel and made pointed remarks about the dryness of the Domestic Repairs business.

Between them they fixed my plate-rack at last so that it would hold "forty jolly dinner services." Said 'Erb as he took my three and sixpence, "That'll outlast you, young man, that will. Firm's a rock, that is."

So I thought when I looked at the job. Evidently 'Erb had charged the odd three shillings for nails.

Three days later those parts of the pink plaster which were still intact began to blush a rosy red.

The patch spread rapidly, and suspecting damp, I telephoned to the landlord. Next morning a plumber arrived, but before he could get to work the plate-rack had to come down.

Without even removing his coat, that highly efficient plumber lifted the rack from the nails on which it rested, and said, "Hope you don't put anything valuable in that!" ("Firm's a rock, that is!" Oh, 'Erb!)

With the removal of each bunch of three-inch nails, more and more plaster pattered into the sink, but one nail gave a little more trouble.

It came away at last in a pair of pincers. Followed a beautiful jet of water, which smote the plumber in the face.

He dodged, and with the removal of his obstructing features the jet shot to the ceiling, and continued to spout steadily, while the plumber groped for a towel, and delivered a rapid and comprehensive monologue.

When he could see again he quickly plugged the hole with a match, and declared that his was a dry job. Something moist and strengthening having been supplied the next business was to sweat a patch over the leak. Then, for sixpence, a cigarette, and the mixture as before, the plumber fixed the plate-rack again. He drove wooden pegs into the wall, and screwed the contrivance to them, so that now, did I wish to do so, I could safely hang myself on it. Also he mended the broken plaster.

But (and this strikes me as gross ingratitude) he told the landlord all about it. He compared the nail in the pipe with those in the wall, and, not being a jobber, he drew inferences.

Next day I received a letter from the landlord which said:

> Sir (it is "Dear Sir" just before quarter day)—the leak in the water pipe was caused by you or someone employed by you, driving a nail into the pipe when fixing your plate-rack.

And now I am waiting for his bill. I could send it to 'Erb, of course, but then he is not a rich man, and he might offer to work off the amount in domestic repairs.

The War of the Roses

The absurd hour at which the sun climbs over the rim of our suburb these days, and the equally preposterous time at which it goes off duty, are together responsible for the fact that I have not seen my garden since last Sunday.

As I write, I do not know whether my lawn (twelve by eight) is under water or not; and I am a little anxious as to the fate of my roses and the four packets of seeds, with such hopeful pictures on their wrappers, which I interred long ago in my Colombian cold frame. (This variety of frame is imported from the Fraser River, B.C., and bears the words "Finest Tinned Salmon." I bought it at the grocer's for fourpence.)

My almanac, which has proved fairly accurate so far, tells me that to-morrow the sun will rise at 7h. 58m., setting at 4h. 23m.

So if I hurry I may be able to have a quick run round to-morrow.

Since I began to own a garden, this Sunday morning inspection has developed into a ceremony, for the ritual of which I am indebted to the man next door and a knot hole in the fence.

After breakfast it is my custom to put on a pair of tremendous boots, roll up my shirt-sleeves and trouser-legs, and sally out with spade and hoe, whistling "The Farmer's Boy." For an hour or two I dig my hardest wherever there is nothing showing above the soil; stopping at intervals to bend my back into the perpendicular again.

And the things I find! The late tenants of my house seemed to have lived upon salmon and pineapple.

This week-end display of energy has another object than mere floriculture. There is the man next door. He must be impressed.

He spends hours in his garden, putting in sticks mostly, and altering his mind. At 10 a.m. he puts a stick in, say a yard North by East of the dustbin.

Then he lights a pipe and paces the path in deep thought. At 10.30 a.m. he takes the stick out again, and drives it in somewhere else. One of his sticks, I know, has been all round the garden twice.

He digs holes and fills them up again when he is not moving sticks; and there is always a business-like strand of rafia hanging out of one of his pockets.

He does these apparently absurd things as if he knew something about the subject, and I am afraid of him. I must get some sticks and watch him closely.

So far our acquaintance has not progressed beyond the nodding stage, but I seem to know the man. He is one of those successful amateur gardeners who take their best blooms to the office every morning in the summer, and flaunt them before their fellow-workers.

They are the worst of bores, these amateurs; and the annoying part of it is that, judging by the buttonholes they wear in the summer, they appear to know something about their hobby.

I happened to mention in the train a month or so ago that I had a garden, and that it was waist-high with thistles and other rank growth. I said I wanted a lawn, and immediately seven men began to explain how to get rid of the weeds and how to grow grass.

Some were for weed-killers, and others for trenching; some were for turf, and others for grass seed; and in five minutes they were all but fighting.

On another occasion I asked what one paid for roses, and how to put them in. Within five minutes friendships of long-standing were being wrecked before my eyes; the solo party in the corner had scattered their cards on the floor and the air was full of mutual recriminations and wild talk about third dormant buds.

When the dust had subsided there was only one thing on which they were all agreed—that I should never grow roses. Years of tribulation lay ahead of me, summer after summer of dreary disappointment; from which cleansing fire, given the requisite courage and persistence, I might one day emerge with a rose "such as I showed you fellows last August."

They talked to me lovingly of mulch and mildew and blight, and of the devouring aphides. Then they laughed, and one by one invited me to their homes to see and hear how it really should be done.

Their bumptious attitude annoyed me, as does the quiet confidence of the man next door, and I decided that something must be done.

By hook or by crook I must have a rose as big as a pickling cabbage, or an aphis like a lobster, to take with me to the City next summer. Else I shall have to travel "third," for I cannot stand their sympathy.

To my assistance came Mr. Perryman, and now my border is rich with promise of roses. At present there is nothing more than a dozen or so of bare twigs, green and reddish brown. But I know them for right roses by the labels and the thorns.

The cardboard labels look awfully engaging, blowing about in the wind and battling to and fro. Somehow they remind me of Kew and the Botanic Gardens.

Labels in a garden look very imposing, especially if there be a sprinkling of Latin on them. In my cold frame, for instance, there is a little wooden tombstone to the memory of some *Correopsis Grandiflora*.

These should be as big as sunflowers at the very least.

But even if my roses never bloom, I shall still derive much satisfaction from the perusal of their name-plates.

For the titles are every bit as dainty as ever the flowers can hope to be; and my plants will have to put their best root forward if they aspire to equal the pictures I have conjured up from their names.

The green stems that climb the trellis are a rambler, "Meg Merrilies," which, of course, will be a wild, dark flower, with a brown eye.

Caroline Testout must be tall, well shaped, and aristocratic; Eugenie Lamesch, I am afraid, will turn out a rather frail creature, delicate and ethereal. She will die young, of consumption for preference; and then Captain Hayward, her sturdy, thick-set, and devoted lover, will commit suicide by green fly.

Farther down is that high-born dame, Madame Pernet Ducher, still a little proud of her ankle and her lineage; while Maman Cochet, the dear buxom old thing, and Frau Karl Druschki, the plump widow of the proprietor of the Delicatessen shop, nestle close together in the corner.

So I am relying on the red and green twigs to uphold the honour of their beautiful names, and, as Mr. Perryman puts it, to "do me proud."

I want to be able to enter my train in the morning with confidence, to gaze scornfully at my fellow-passengers from behind my buttonhole. And I want to gain the respect of the man next door.

At present he only smiles indulgently when I walk round and read my labels, but we will show him yet.

I am leaving the mulch and the mildew and the third dormant buds to Mr. Perryman, and shall content myself with the pursuit of the green fly every Sunday morning.

But, like all amateur gardeners, I shall keep these details from the men in the train.

The Leather Boxes

Whatever the copybook may say, punctuality must be counted as one of the meaner virtues; and they who practise it are for the most part driven thereto by necessity.

To impress us with its importance in the scheme of things, and to boom its beauty, catch-phrases, the work of an early advertisement writer, have been invited. These are known as proverbs, signposts pointing to the road of wealth.

Left to themselves, few right-thinking men would count punctuality among the virtues at all; but there are trains, and other punctual people who will not wait, and there are employers.

It is a combination of these three circumstances which for the last month has driven me from my cosy bed to catch the 7.3 a.m.

I am not quite sure whether the train I catch is the 7.3 or the 7.11; anyway, it is the first train that comes in after I arrive at the station; and it is somewhere in the middle of the night, before even the lark has thought about tuning up for his early orchestral business.

This train is a "workmen's" (which means that I lose 1s. 6d. a week on my season ticket), and it is full of the victims of punctuality; women and men, girls and boys, who if they are two minutes behind the hooter lose a "quarter."

But they are always there, always in the same seats in the same compartments, and so regularly have I caught this train, on and off, that I am beginning to know them.

Usually I sit next to the girl in the grey tweed costume and the blue hat. We are quite old friends, and yesterday morning as I walked to my seat I thought she smiled a little in salutation. Conceit on my part, maybe, but there it is.

The young people who catch the "workmen's" are much more interesting than their later sisters of the 9.20. These latter work in offices and hide themselves behind newspapers throughout the journey.

For the most part, the early-risers alight at Aldersgate-street, where the blouse and corset factories are, and they do not read newspapers much.

Travelling with them morning after morning, I have noticed that nine out of every ten of them carry a little leather dispatch box; a flat, brown thing with a handle, two locks that click, and usually three initials.

These boxes have roused in me a devilish curiosity. I cannot read my paper for them. All down each side of the carriage they stretch, laid in the laps of their owners, all alike, mysterious. What do these workgirls want with little leather boxes, usually considered sacred to the legal profession?

Once upon a time a Dorothy bag, with two cords by which to hang it over one's arm, was considered large enough to hold the tiny handkerchief and the purse and the butterscotch of the City girl.

But now she must have a dispatch box, with her initials on its side.

My neighbour the girl in the grey tweed, she has one; and it bears the letters M. E. B. I think her name must be Margaret, one of the "five sweet symphonies." She has the fine nose and chin of a Margaret.

Now, occasionally she has to open her little box, but before she does so she darts a furtive look at me. Of course, I am deep in the leading article, but oh! how I want to look.

One or two things that I know of I could not help seeing. There is the red-covered copy of "Lorna Doone," which she reads steadily every morning, and closes with a long breath at King's Cross.

That comes out of the box and goes back, but the lid is only lifted just so much and no more. Then there is her wee handkerchief with M. E. B. in its corner, and her purse wherein is her ticket, and a small green bottle of, I think, smelling-salts.

All these I have seen because I could not help it. They have been wanted on the journey.

But what else is there? What, besides toilet accessories, is in all those other little boxes?

Some, I know, contain knitting needles and balls of wool, and crochet cotton.

There is A. L. P. two or three seats away; she has been working these ten days on a Peter Pan collar, and I have watched the wheel-like pattern grow morning by morning under her nimbly flying fingers. In and out and over and over goes the thread, and between Hammersmith and Edgware-road half a spoke is added to the wheel.

Further along—and I only see her when some stranger steals my place beside the girl in grey tweed—sits J. H., click-clicking away with two long bone needles and some thick Berlin wool. Before the cold weather has gone somebody will be the richer by a nice warm "comforter."

See her lips move to the needles as she works. "Two purl, one plain, drop one, two plain, make one"; then there is something wrong, and the stitches have to be counted along the needle.

Then comes her station, the work is rolled round the needles, the loose wool is wound up again, and the whole bundled into the little box, not to come out again, maybe, until the homeward journey.

But the tatting, or knitting, or crochet work does not fill these little boxes, even when helped out by "The Shadow of Ashlydyat," or a thicker library volume.

There must be something else, and I suspect sandwiches, with perhaps an occasional little pie-dish.

Opposite myself and M. E. B. there sits as a rule a girl of about 14, with two long pigtails down her back and a cold nose like a half-ripe cherry.

She reads pale pink novelettes—nearly one a day, for the titles are always changing—and as she reads she knocks her heels together to keep her young blood on the move.

Being only a youngster, she has no little leather box as yet, but none the less I am extremely interested in her.

I want to know why she catches the seven-something every morning, rubbing her eyes and yawning behind her four-by-four square of muslin.

Girls with two pigtails and skirts reaching ever so little below their knees have no business catching workmen's trains, their dreams half finished.

In one great thing do these early morning workwomen differ from the City girls in the later trains; they talk to one another but little.

The 9.20 is full of laughter and chatter; and some of its passengers talk politics. But there are no politics in the seven-something; only silent concentration on the matter in hand, be it reading or knitting or crochet-work.

The business-like gloom of the factory or workroom is over them all. They forget that for those few minutes of the day at least they are free agents; and so they work or read steadily on until within a few minutes of their stations.

Then, as if by instinct, they lift their heads, close their books, roll up the knitting, and put them ever so gingerly into their little leather boxes, mighty careful not to raise the lids too far.

The Blue Minuet

He stands on my mantelpiece, between the Nang Tsu ginger-jar and the little soapstone God of Content; a dapper little fellow in long coat and knee breeches of blue and white, an undoubted "Gentleman of the Period."

Here and there, on his buttons, his garters, and the frill of his stock, you may see traces of bright gold; the rest long since scrubbed off by some energetic housewife.

Where he came from I have not the remotest idea, except that his pedigree handed down through a century or more, mentions him as having been a wedding present from mother to daughter through four or five generations.

Stamped beneath his feet are a small red diamond and the number 11374 in quaint figures, curiously entwined; but whether he be Dresden or Chelsea or Capo di Monte I cannot tell. He may be worth fourpence or forty pounds; I care little, so he be beautiful.

And beautiful he is, from the crown of his blue-ribboned peruke to the soles of his little shoes.

There is a hint of nice breeding about the poise of him, his head slightly bent in graceful salutation, his fingers resting on his hips, coats pushed back, and his right foot raised in the first step of the dainty minuet.

See how he "makes a leg," arching the instep to throw out the muscle of the calf; and by the confident smile on his mouth you may know that he is perfectly satisfied with the result.

To-day as I look at him I think his smile is a little sweeter than it seemed to me a month ago.

He has stood beside the soapstone god for a year now, always shaping for the opening movement, always waiting for his partner in the dance. Sometimes I have thought he tried to stretch his neck ever such a little, to peer round the ginger-jar for a glimpse of her.

How long he has stood thus waiting, on how many mantelpieces, I do not know; but we may picture him going from home to home, from mother to daughter, always bowing and pushing his coats back, ready to greet his lost fair with a smile.

That there had been such a partner I felt quite certain, but that he would ever meet her again I doubted.

Yet he did, a month ago; and it was I that brought them together.

We had both long given her up. The shards of her, I told him, were deep in some suburban garden, her head decorated a rockery; or she had been ground to clay once more, to help in the building of a mineral water factory. Still he only smiled and peered round the ginger-jar.

"If she has missed those things," I said to him over a pipe one night, "if she be not bricks and mortar, she has been turned into light and heat in a municipal dust destructor."

Yet, he never flinched, but lifted his foot, and bowed his head, making ready for the viol and flute.

I found her on a stall in Shoreditch, flanked on one side by a "Pilgrim's Progress" and a "Serious Call," and on the other by some stair rods, a spirit level, and a pewter mug. Over her head a naphtha lamp roared, and gave out filthy fumes; and her back was all splashed from the mire of the passing traffic.

With a little too much haste I picked her up and glanced quickly at the mark beneath her feet. There was the small red diamond, but no number that I could see. That mattered little; her left foot was tilted, her panniers ever so slightly raised for the opening bar, and on my mantelpiece her lover waited.

"Two bob," said the man behind the stall, and I put her in my breast pocket.

According to the rules of the game I should have haggled, offered eighteen pence, walked away without her, and eventually compromised for one and ninepence.

"Excuse me, sir," said the salesman, "but which is it you've taken?" (There was only one on the stall, only one in the wide world.)

"Oh, sir! That one. Oh! I begs your pardon, sir, that one's three bob. That's real Sevvers, that is. Three bob, and thank you, sir. If I 'ad the pair of 'em it'd be 'arf-a-jimmy the two."

Would it, indeed? thought I and cuddled her to me as I paid.

Four times I took her out in the train, and got a lot of the grime off her with my handkerchief before we arrived home. Then with hot water and a soft brush I cleaned her of the Shoreditch mire, and laid her beauty bare.

There is no doubt about her being his partner; the blue flowers on her white farthingale tell me that. Then there are faint traces of gold on her laced stomacher, and the blue bow on her head-dress.

Her head, too, is saucily bent forward, and the taper fingers pick at her pannier as she gets ready to curtsey. The little Cupid's bow of her mouth still carries its rosy colouring, and on her cheek is the faintest of blushes, a little deeper now, perhaps, than when I found her.

But what of her wanderings up and down in the world, the lonely years since she was torn from the side of her partner? Think of her journeyings from pillar to post, from her lowly home to some still lowlier pawnshop, to wait in vain beside marble clocks and blankets and cheap cutlery; until by some pass she came to the stall in Shoreditch and to me.

I was a little afraid lest in her years of waiting her beauty should have faded. Perhaps under the mud her nose was chipped or her hair disarranged. But soon she stood out in all her perfect grace, lightly poised on one foot, with hair massed in shapely rolls and in right order, and her raised hoops showing an ankle that time had not robbed of its trim neatness.

Maybe I scrubbed her a little too eagerly, but when she was rinsed there was an eyebrow missing. That I mended with a fine brush and some Indian ink, so that she was now all he could wish her, and I dried her before the fire.

Though it upset the balance of things, I placed her close against her partner, on the same side of the Nang Tsu ginger-jar. Then I left the room.

As I closed the door behind me I thought I heard the tinkle of china.

The Lamp-Post

Not far from my garden gate there lives an old blackguard of a rooster, a strutting, full-chested humbug, whose business it is to knock up the sun each morning.

That there shall be no hitch in the proceedings, he starts his shrill clarion about one hour after midnight. With head well back and beak stretched wide he splits the night in twain with his hoarse yell.

But nothing happens. Maybe a hen, snug on the perch above, tells him in a tired voice to come back to bed, and not to make an ass of himself.

Presently he tries again, half a tone higher this time; and still it remains dark as the Pit.

Well, he has done his best, and if the whole jolly solar system chooses to miss its appointments you must not lay it to his charge. With which he flaps his wings three times, to signify that he washes his hands of the business, struts a little, and blunders upstairs to his perch again.

As 2 a.m. he repeats the whole performance, and thence at irregular intervals all through the otherwise stilly night.

But see him when the East is really grey, when a chimney-pot or two are sending up the fumes from the breakfast rasher. There is triumph in his trumpet now.

"I told you so," he says to the admiring hens. "You know, when I start it's bound to come off, and there it is." Out goes his chest, up comes his right leg, slowly, toes spread, knee back and close against the body; and down again by easy stages to the dust. Again with the left leg, and he has covered six inches in as many seconds.

Would you not walk like that if you were responsible for the daylight of a hemisphere?

After a week of it I shifted my bedroom to the front of the house. He was not alone responsible for this; there were his friends spread all up and down the country from Brompton to Berwick-on-Tweed.

He would crow first, waking the rooster three hundred yards away, who would crow and wake the next in the chain, and so through Hampstead and Potter's Bar to Peterborough and the Black Country; till the high blare on Skiddaw roused the roosters of Carlisle.

Then the cocks of the North, finding how they had been misled, shouted opprobrious epithets down the long line to my friend at the end of the road, who naturally answered back. And I used to hear it all.

So I trundled my bed into the next room, and for three nights slept without interruption.

Beneath my new bedroom window there stands a street lamp; and I had not occupied my fresh quarters a week before I discovered that in the glow of this lamp the local lovers met and said their fond good-nights; that here, and here only, could men promise at inordinate length to see one another on the following evening.

It was the pump round which the village gossips gathered to exchange views and talk scandal.

Lying in my bed near the open window, I overhear between ten o'clock and midnight snatches of recipes for vegetable marrow jam, the reason why the speaker missed that easy red loser, long arguments for and against municipal trading (I shall be driven into leaning out of the window and joining in one of these nights), a sprinkling of fond kisses, occasional hiccoughs, and many injunctions not to be late in the morning.

One incident of ten minutes' duration happens nearly every night. Two women draw near to the lamp-post, talking volubly. Stopping beneath my window, says one:

"Well, I must leave you now. Good-night, dear."

"Good-night, dear," says the second. "See you to-morrow." They part, and I hear the footsteps of the first pattering along until she reaches No. 7.

Then, "Give my love to Bert," she calls.

"All right," from across the road.

Again at No. 11 the first stops.

"And Jim and Suey," she shouts.

"All right," says a weak voice a hundred yards away.

A pause; then from far up the road:

"And Young Alfie."

"All right," from behind the church this time.

Here follows an interval of perhaps a minute and a half, during which, I suppose, the first speaker runs through the tables of affinity.

At the end of the road she stops once more, and adds at the top of her voice, "And remember me to Aunt Harriet."

"All right," very faintly from across the green.

I am beginning to look forward to that bit, but there are some things I hear which annoy me, either because I cannot get interested in them, or because they are incomplete.

What is it to me that Miss What's-her-name waits after choir practice because Mr. Thingmebob lives in her direction? What do I care if a blouse like Mary's can be made from four yards of double-width art serge at eleven-three?

Nor does it thrill me to know that the last half ton of coal was nearly all slate, "and I'm going to let him know about it when he comes again."

There was the beetroot, too. That kept me wondering for a good hour one night last week.

"Good-night, Aunt," said Eva.

"Good-night, Eva," said aunt.

Then, from about four doors up, aunt turned and called, "Eva! Eva, dear! Don't forget to bring the beetroot, will you?"

"All right, Auntie," said Eva, and the rest was silence, with a flaming interrogation mark across it.

Was it a picnic, a harvest festival, or does Eva take her own salads with her when she goes out to dine? It is still troubling me, but I am hoping for further revelations on some future occasion. Perhaps auntie will give the show away one night from four doors up.

This kind of thing lasts until a little after midnight, by which time a full eight hours' sleep are impossible for me. So I lie and listen to the soft squelch of the policeman's rubber soles, and watch for the glow of his bull's-eye to flash across my window.

Last night, when all the farewells had been said, the front doors all bolted, and the dogs all called indoors, I was just dozing, and the first milk-barrow clanked round the corner. So I got up and dressed.

On the whole, I think the fowls are to be preferred. Their conversation rouses no curiosity. Whereas now I am kept worrying about other people's affairs, teething babies, crochet designs, the washing of flannels, the sacking of "generals," and rural depopulation.

Then there is auntie's beetroot. I wonder if Eva remembered it.

The Feud

The man at the greengrocer's is a bachelor, and, he will tell you, "proud of it." His views on womenfolk are striking, and deserve to be placed on record.

"Been a bachelor all my life," he says, "and likely so to remain. Cooks for myself, washes for myself, and keeps my own place ship-shape by myself. Won't have a female in the place. Can't abear 'em … Three pound tuppence them, lady; four pound threepence these.

"They're like beadles, they are. Like cockroaches. Once get 'em in the 'ouse and you never get 'em out again … Seven pound for sixpence, lady, them nice liddle picklin' onions … Never get 'em out again. Like beadles they are, an' ants."

Of one woman at least (she is thirteen, but old for her years) I know this to be true. You may remember Gloria.

Because I had made a good breakfast and felt virtuous in consequence, and because her hands were cold and her nose red, I contracted with Gloria to clean the step at sixpence a week and a piece of cake.

To that arrangement she kept for a fortnight; then behold her in the kitchen, kneeling on a chair, cleaning the knives, to Mendelssohn's "Sleep, Gentle Babe," which she learns at school.

A week later, "Please I've spilt some 'ar'stoney water on the lid of the coal cellar." By some feminine instinct she knew just where to find the blacklead brushes, and now that little job has become part of her recognised duties. So I am mulcted in eightpence a week now, and a larger piece of cake.

I am afraid Gloria talks—brags—about me a little, for the Saturday after she joined the staff another girl called at nine o'clock, Gloria's time being ten, and offered to do the step for fourpence.

The following week she came again, and I was obliged to tell her that I had already made other arrangements. She looked disparagingly at Gloria's semicircular smears, sniffed, and said, "Yes, I know; but I'll clean it for fourpence, properly. Not streaky, like that."

Five minutes after she had gone Gloria arrived. Usually she dives beneath the sink for her pail and flannel, but this morning she stood nervously wringing imaginary water out of her "tammy."

" 'As another girl bin 'ere 'smornin'?" she asked. I nodded.

"Girl with black 'air, bigger'n me?"

"Yes," I said.

"Come after my situation?" she went on.

"She wished to clean the step," I admitted.

"Girl with ear-rings?" Yes, she wore ear-rings—gold crescent moons.

"Sort of a gyppo?" Well, she certainly was dark, and rather handsome.

"Wanted to do it for less'n I get?" Yes, for twopence less.

"Oh, did she?" and Gloria planked her pail into the sink and turned on the water.

When she brought the pail back the subject was reopened. That gyppo kid was 15, and only in the fourth standard, and not fit even to be there. Could not say her "nine times" dodging.

Her father drove a barge for the sawmills. She, Gloria, had no father, and, therefore, hers was the bigger claim on my step. Further, the gyppo could not clean steps for toffee.

The next week the dark girl came again to see if I had changed my mind, and Gloria, arriving a little earlier than usual, was just in time to see her competitor disappearing round the corner.

She drew four long turquoise hat pins from her "tammy," laid all on the copper, and said, "Shan't be a jiffy."

In ten minutes she was back again, breathing hard, and flushed as to the face.

"Bet she don't come 'ere any more," she said, and sucked vigorously at the ball of her thumb.

"What have you done?" I asked, a little scared.

"Flopped 'er," said Gloria. "Flopped her properly. Tried to bite me, she did. They don't know 'ow to fight fair, them gyppos. I give 'er bite!"

The excitement over, Gloria presently wept into her pail, and wrung out the cloth to dry her eyes. That over, I spoke to her sternly on the matter of the fight.

If she wished to keep her place there must be no more "flopping." She must bear herself as became the hired domestic of a respectable householder. Why, the man next door was a churchwarden, and what would he think?

"But, if she follers me round tryin' to sneak my jobs, can't I go for her?"

"Not while you work for me," I said as sternly as I knew how. I myself would speak seriously to the dark girl if I got an opportunity, but in the neighbourhood of my house, at least, there must be no fighting.

"Think of my neighbours, and the people across the road," I said.

"I'll cop 'er at school," said Gloria. "I'll cop 'er, an' I'll learn 'er."

But the dark girl was a persevering young person. If she could not get the job for herself, she would at least spoil it for Gloria.

So she waited until her rival had left, with her mouth full of cake, and then she rang the bell, standing with both feet on my immaculate step. And it is my private opinion that she had previously mired her boots for that purpose.

"Can I clean your step, sir?" she asked, and turned not an eyelash in the asking.

Here was my chance to read her my lesson on the evils of price-cutting and fair fighting.

"It has already been cleaned," I began, but before I could get any further the gyppo glanced down at her own muddy tracks, and smiled ever so gently.

"Oh, 'as it?" she said, and laughed consumedly.

The Passion-Flower

It is hard to be abrupt with anyone who calls you "Sonny"; especially when the person in question is a dear, wrinkled old soul with merry eyes, who only hicks a goffered white frill to be a real "Head of an Old Woman" by Rembrandt.

"Good morning, sonny," she said, and before the automatic "Not to-day, thank you" had jumped to my lips she had swung her basket on to the step, where it overlapped just enough to prevent the door being shut.

"A liddle weskit," she said, "or a liddle pair o' trousis, sonny? Just you think if there ain't a liddle weskit what you've done with, or a liddle pair o' trousis. I'd just love to do a stroke of business with you, I would. You've got a lucky face, you 'ave, sonny. Just you think."

I thought for a space, but not about my wardrobe. I thought of this wrinkled dame, seventy at least, toiling through the suburbs all day, with her great basket of gimcrack china and her huge sack of "cast-offs"; struggling from door to door, and capturing perhaps one waistcoat in a hundred doors.

It was bitter cold in the doorway, and yet, when she had put her basket on the step, she drew her bare brown arm across her forehead and wiped it down her apron.

Under her nodding bonnet I could see that her hair was grey and thin, and the corners of her eyes were all wrinkled as if in frozen laughter; wrinkles that spoke of years of battling against the weather with her two great loads.

Even at the end of her day's work there were her burdens still, the one a trifle lighter, may be, but the other considerably heavier. For where she gains a pair of trousers she loses but a pair of vases or an art flowerpot.

"You 'ave a look, sonny. There's sure to be a liddle old coat or something what's seen its best days. Something what'll do me a bit of good, and you won't miss it."

Yes, there certainly was such a coat upstairs, I remembered; a coat that had gone through all the stages that a decent coat can expect to see.

Its first appearance as a "best" I have forgotten, it was so long ago. Its existence as an "every-day," I remember well, and later its descent to the "knock-about" stage, the happiest in its career.

I had loafed in it, smoked in it, and pottered about the garden in it; its lining hung in shreds, its sleeves were all frayed at the edges, and its place in my affections had been taken by another. Altogether I should be rather glad to rid myself of it.

"You don't leave 'em off till you've done with 'em, do you, sonny?" She held the garment up by the collar, found all its imperfections with her twinkling eyes, searched each closely, and looked up at me. Under cover of her examination, as she twisted and turned it, her free hand groped for, found, and explored the pockets one after another.

I could have saved her that trouble.

A few minutes before I had been through them thoroughly, to discover a shrivelled tulip bulb and some bent nails.

I think the old lady was a little disappointed, both with the condition of the garment and the contents of its pockets. For she began now to depreciate my property, to handle it gingerly, with a lively contempt in the upward curl of her lip.

" 'Taint exactly what you'd call a coat—not now—is it, sonny?" she said. "Sort of done in, ain't it?" Her quick little eyes flitted from the odd buttons to the enlarged button-holes, from the ragged lining to the torn elbow.

"It was a fine piece of Harris tweed, once," I pointed out.

"Once!" she said, in such a tone that I felt downright ashamed of myself.

"What d'you want for it, sonny?" she asked presently. "Here's a nice liddle pair of vases. Real Majolica, those are. Worth I don't know 'ow much. Or this liddle art pot for a fern, very 'an'some. Or a candle-stick with a motter about early to bed on it. Or 'ere's a pair of 'an'some egg cups with pictures of the King and Queen ... No?

"Well, now, sonny, 'ow about a flower? A liddle castor-oil plant. My young man's down the street with the plants, an' 'e's got castor-oil an' injia-rubber, an' stone-crop, an' loads of others with foreign names.

"Tell you what, sonny. 'E's got a passion-flower, a 'an'some liddle plant. Grows anywheres! What d'you say to a liddle passion-flower? I'll run and get it. You look after my bundles."

And so for five minutes I stood on my doorstep with a huge basket full of gaudy art pottery, and a sack full of other people's cast clothes.

Certainly, I thought, a passion-flower would be preferable to the pink and green Majolica ware, or the frantic fern pots. It would look rather nice climbing over the trellis.

She returned, panting, with a ball of mould in her hand, from which protruded a black stem with one or two pale green buds. It might have been anything, so to be on the safe side I threw doubt on its right to be classed as a passion-flower.

"Well, sonny," she said, "my young man says 'e believes it's a passion-flower, or—or something like that. Something foreign, 'e said, with 'ponica' at the end of it. Big blue flower it's got, big as a dahlia. Look a treat in the summer."

Evidently she thought I wanted my coat back, for "Tell you what," she continued, "I'll give you the passion-flower an' a egg-cup with a coloured 'Ampton Court on it."

She plunged the coat into her sack, and swung the great bundle round to her stooping shoulders. Then, with her tinkling basket pulling her sideways, she toddled heavily away.

I planted the passion-flower against the trellis that evening. It has been there a fortnight now. Nothing has happened to it so far. I do not even know if it has a root, and I am beginning to wonder.

But she was such a jolly little body, with such merry eyes that met you fair, so I am hoping for the best.

The Spike-File

My carefully planned time-table lays it down that Thursday evening is to be devoted to work. Lest I should forget this, and I do try hard sometimes, I have made a practice of entering the fact on an "Engagement" tablet which came to me on a birthday long ago; one of those washable china things which one keeps in excellent order for a fortnight and then consults about once a month.

There it stands now; its pathetic legend reading:

Monday, Jan. 6, B'lld H'cap. 150.
Thursday, Jan. 9, work.

The first engagement I remember well. I pointed out to the handicapper how absurd it was to put me on the 150 mark. Why, the other man—but never mind now.

Whether or not I kept the second appointment, and worked on Thursday, January 9, I have now no means of knowing.

Most probably I went to my room, lit the lamp, tilted the shade, sat at my desk, and said, "Let's see."

Then for maybe half an hour I messed about with the papers on the spike-file, taking them off one by one, and saying, "That must be done, and that must be done"; tore up one or two old letters, answered another, jammed the "must-be-done" papers back on the file again, and picked up a book.

I think I must often have spent my Thursday evening in that manner, for the file is nearly full now of things that really ought to be done, and the top paper has seven separate holes in it. One of these evenings I must go for it, and clear the lot off.

I do not blame myself alone for this seeming lack of resolution. There is another person concerned, to wit, the girl next door. (That long-drawn "A—ah!" is quite uncalled for, sir.)

When I first dedicated my Thursday evenings to work I reckoned without that lady. And Thursday evening, it would appear, is her evening "off."

No sooner do I plant myself at my desk, with that virtuous "now for a good evening's work" feeling, than she starts on the piano.

Richard Wagner, it seems, is her favourite composer, and even that master of cacophony would be astonished at her rendering of the Prelude to Act III. of "Lohengrin."

Lacking a trombone, an instrument somewhat prominent in that selection, she punches the bass notes like fury, her fingers stretched to cover an octave, and her right foot jabbing all the time at the loud pedal. The twiddley bits for the strings she supplies from the other end of the keyboard in staccato jerks, prestissimo.

The resulting clamour is evidently to her liking, for she plays it twice, and the second performance is even better than the first; louder, that is.

You should see the china shepherdess on my mantelpiece dancing to it. On an average Thursday evening she often shifts as much as a couple of inches nearer the dreadful edge. She will dance herself into the fender one evening, and then I shall knock and complain.

It is quite a recognised thing on Fridays for me to spend a quarter of an hour putting pictures straight. Sometimes I think the landlord ought to be told. You see, we stand on gravel, and one never knows.

Up to the present I have not, to my knowledge, set eyes on my musical neighbour, but I have often admired the strength of her right forearm.

The second half of the performance, from which I have learned the sex of the artist, is vocal, and lasts about half an hour. It begins with Elizabeth's Prayer, rendered in what I believe is known as the "bel canto" style, a relic of the Italian school.

On the final note of the climax you stamp your left foot heavily on the ground and raise your right hand to heaven, much as a policeman regulates traffic.

Next comes half an hour of exercises, musical fireworks, Czerny's *Etude de la Vélocité*, I think.

That is when I plunge my papers on to the spike-file once more, and walk up and down the room trying to keep my temper. One evening I started an opposition show with the "Bandelero," and—well, you know, I can't sing a little bit. But I swamped Elizabeth's Prayer, and the shepherdess collided with a brass candlestick in her excitement.

But it was of no use. I had no sooner finished the last note of that brave ballad than from the piano next door thundered the "Bandelero," as it should be sung.

Evidently my neighbour has a sense of humour, and I should like to meet her. I think we might arrange a compromise. But I wish she would not "tremolo" on her top notes; it sounds like jelly.

Once I very nearly did see her. It was a Saturday afternoon, and I was pottering round the garden, which is separated from hers by a high wall. It is about eight feet high, I think, and I am only—well, I am not eight feet.

Suddenly what proved later to be a paper model of an aeroplane came sailing over the wall, swam about a little, and dropped on my garden. I picked it up and essayed to throw it back. Three times it darted upwards, swerved, and volplaned to the grass again, and at the fourth attempt, also a failure, I heard a giggle from behind the wall.

Quickly I clambered on to the dustbin, the toy in my hand, and a polite "Is this yours?" on my lips. But she had gone.

If she can play with paper aeroplanes in the garden, she ought not to be more than fourteen. Yet no child of such tender years ever had sufficient strength to render that beastly Prelude with such vigour and verve.

I wonder what she is like. A merry, light-hearted soul, I should think. I hear her in the morning sometimes—washing up. As a rule she sings "Always," or "Sometimes," or "Never," or "For Ever," some pathetic drawing-room ballad with plenty of tears and tremolos in it, when she is washing up. And she sings them with such a merry lilt in her voice. I really must get to know her somehow.

The Quarrel

All unknown to the principals I have been witness during the last few days of a quaint duel of wits and words. The combatants I have not yet set eyes upon, but from the evidence at my command I should put their ages at something between ten and thirteen years, and their gender I know to be feminine.

The proceedings were opened early in the week by Miss Annie Boddy and a piece of chalk. Annie, I suspect, has "ginger" hair, for her share of the contests seems to have had more than a touch of temper about it.

When I arrived home on Tuesday evening the first shot had been fired. Across the pavement in front of the local grocer's shop there ran the legend in a fine bold hand, "Gert Page is a sopy kid."

Beneath this was a Neolithic drawing of something having a rude likeness to a human being, a circle for its head, a triangle for its trunk, and a collection of garden rakes and toasting-forks for arms and legs.

The face was bisected by a tremendous mouth, rectangular and over-crowded with teeth; the nose was bulbous, and about the goggle eyes was a suggestion of astigmatism.

This then was Gert. It was an interesting libel, terse and to the point, marred neither by circumlocution nor digression; and the drawing which accompanied it was no less direct and ruthless in its striving after truth.

There it stood, telling all who read that Gert was a "sopy kid," that by this picture the world might know and recognise her for what she was, a triangular-trunked horror.

On the next evening I noticed an alteration in the impeachment.

The name of Gert had been ruled out, and that of Annie Boddy written above. Evidently Mistress Page had seen the denunciation of herself, and to save chalk had substituted her enemy's name, leaving the libel as it was. "You're another," said Gert in effect.

As an afterthought she added beneath the whole, "Annie Boddy can't spell"; and that was how I left matters on Thursday morning.

During the day Annie must have called round, and was doubtless highly gratified to learn that her message had reached the person for whom it was intended. So down on her knees she went, and more careful of her orthography this time, added to the charge against Gert, "And a cat." She also rearranged the names, and made the necessary correction in her spelling.

By this time the whole inscription occupied quite two yards of the pavement, and it is still growing. Each morning sees some new phrase or term of opprobrium added to the lengthening charge sheet; each evening sees the morning's work undone. It is like a red-hot by-election.

So far my sympathies are all with Gert; I am on her side. For her part in the campaign has been conducted in an orderly and decent manner. Spitfire methods she leaves to her rival, and contents herself with crisp criticism of Annie's somewhat neglected education.

The latter young lady, on the other hand, has more than once had recourse to the phrase "up the pole," and one of her most recent efforts necessitated the use of the word "balmy."

Fearful of the lash of her opponent's chalk-stick, Annie evidently thought more than was good for her about the correct spelling of that word. Twice it has been altered, once from "balmy" to "barmy," and again back to its original form. And now for the life of me I cannot say which is correct.

"Balmy" we know means soft and gentle, when applied to breezes, for instance; and something similar is suggested by its application to persons alleged to be mentally deficient.

But consider Annie's alternative spelling. Barmy means containing barm, and barm is the product of fermentation. It is also used to make dough spongy and like unto the grey matter of the village idiot. (Or does the term come from the Barmecide Prince who provided that strange dinner for the beggar?)

I am wondering how long the battle will continue. Either the chalk will run out or the quarrel will go on right up the street and round the corner. There is another thing I wish to know. Does Annie lurk about in doorways or behind lamp-posts to see the effect of her work on Gert? And does Gert hide herself in the neighbourhood to see Annie squirm?

It is an unsatisfactory business slanging an opponent if you cannot see the results of your efforts.

That is what I always think about another anonymous writer whose work one meets almost every day. He is the humorist who alters the inscriptions in railway carriages. Under the rack you will read "To eat Six." That is his handiwork, and he travels all up and down the country with a full stock of sharp penknives, perpetuating that jest, always choosing an empty carriage, where he can do his work without hindrance.

Sometimes he varies the entertainment by scratching out a letter from the plate on the door, so that the alighting passenger is advised to "Wait Until the rain Stops." How he must roar to himself as he does it.

Now, both a joke and an insult lose a deal of their point unless the perpetrator is witness of the effect they produce. The railway humorist could hardly resist the temptation to ride in a full carriage, with furtive eyes peeping from behind his newspaper, waiting anxiously for somebody to chuckle at his jest.

So it must be with Annie and Gert, I think. Each must hide somewhere in the shadows when the other arrives to read the real truth about herself.

The only thing I am afraid of is that the two will meet face to face one day, and I shall come home to find the pavement littered with hair.

"Poddles"

She is one of those young persons of whom staid grown-ups exclaim, "Why, whatever will she be like when she grows up?"

By the adult standard she is saucy, precocious, devoid of due respect for her elders, dangerously truthful, and a little pretty (but she does not know that yet). Sometimes, when her nether lip protrudes, she is entirely beyond the control of her parents. But if one is careful that need not happen often, and Poddles' parents are very, very careful. She is the most heart-rending tear-distiller I have ever met with.

In case you should not like her, I would hasten to add that I am only her uncle, and that by adoption. Poddles adopted me, and as she already had one father who so far had filled the position fairly well, I was made an uncle.

Being Poddles' uncle is no sinecure, let me tell you; and I often think her father must find his duties a little irksome at times.

Our first meeting happened thus. Poddles stopped me at the gate with, "Please have you got any cigarette pictures, please?" Up to that moment my experience in these matters had been small. So I adopted the "genial old gentleman" attitude.

"Well, my little maid," I said; "I've no doubt we shall be able to find you a cigarette picture somewhere." (Business with pockets, and grandfatherly smile.) "And if I give you one, what will you do with it?"

I thought I was doing this rather well; when, "I'm not little," said Poddles, "and I want the pictures for Tubby. He gives me a ha'penny for ten, and I've got ten now, nearly, all but—all but six."

The next time Poddles waylaid me I gave her my cigarette picture before she asked for it, and took no notice of her. Whereupon, as is the custom with children when you ignore them, she trotted by my side, and in four breathless minutes told me her name, address, occupation of father, date of next party, colour of frock for said party, list of guests, number of varieties of cake, and the name of her mother's domestic's young man. From that date we have known each other intimately.

Once or twice Poddles has allowed me to take her for a walk, on the distinct understanding that I made no attempt to hold her hand, except when crossing the road; and a day or two ago we arranged to go to look at the daffodils and the squirrels.

Our way to the tram lay through a highly respectable road, where street cries are most sternly forbidden, where milkmen wear rubber heels, and hawkers are shot on sight.

In spite of the high blue sky and the blossoming apple-tree outside "Sowerby Towers," where the doctor lives, we were both behaving admirably. Presently my companion put her finger in her mouth, and wobbled it about as she yelled. The result was fine.

Very loud and very clear, "Olly-olly-olly-olly" it said; and the hush that followed was terrifying. Asked why she did it, Poddles replied that she "couldn't help it; she had to do somefing."

Then I knew that I was in for an afternoon of what her mother calls "high spirits."

In the tram we had some more, so that I heartily wished we had walked. Or I should have been satisfied with a placard on my chest, saying: "This is not my child. I am only taking her out for the day, and am in no way responsible for her manners."

Having settled herself comfortably, with her legs sticking straight out in front of her, Poddles began to clap her feet together, a sure sign that she is meditating some evil.

Drawing a long breath, she addressed herself to a large beaded woman who nursed an umbrella in the opposite corner.

What follows is extremely rapid, and devoid of all pauses and punctuation.

"We're going to Kew Gardens and this is my uncle but he isn't my uncle really only we call him that and I'm six and I shall be seven next year and eight next year and I'm nearly eight now and we're going to Kew Gardens."

No sign from the beaded lady. As a rule Poddles doesn't make mistakes, but this time she had drawn a blank.

Close by was a lady with an armful of wallflowers, and as the corners of her mouth showed the beginnings of a smile, Poddles tried her recitative again.

"This is my uncle," she went on, "and we're going to Kew Gardens to see the squirls and—" she looked at me sideways—"and the lions and tigers."

This last was a mistake arising from an excess of enthusiasm; and I knew that unless she were diverted, elephants and giraffes would soon be numbered among the attractions of Kew. So I gave her the coppers for our fares.

"Ooooh! What a big, fat conductor," she shrieked, and clapped her feet merrily together. "Uncle! Unkie!" (I was trying to look as if she belonged to someone else.) "Are you going to pay for me, or shall I have to sit on your lap?" It was the longest and the slowest penny ride I have ever enjoyed.

Presently the wallflower lady caught her eye and encouraged her to further efforts.

"I'm nearly eight," she said; "and I know lots and heaps of poetries. Shall I say you some?

Was a lil sparrow
Wennup a gutter spout
Long came a funderstorm
Washer sparrow out."

All this in a clear, shrill, sing-song, so that I blushed, inwardly as it were, for my tottering dignity. There were further references also to the corpulency of the conductor, while I prayed for the end of the journey.

"My dad's a great big man," she said as we left the car; adding, "this is only my uncle." You've no idea how tiny that sort of thing makes one feel.

In the Gardens she addressed a uniformed attendant who was explaining something to a group of ladies.

"Please where are the squirls?" she asked. "I want to take my uncle to see them." By this time I had dwindled to next to nothing.

Well, we saw the daffodils; and tried, at Poddles' suggestion, to feed a robin with tobacco because we had forgotten the breadcrumbs; and we ran away from a strutting and amorous peacock; and we touched all the things that the labels tell you not to touch; and we walked on the grass edge which on no account are you permitted to walk on; and we picked one late snowdrop in the rock garden. When I say we did these things, I mean that Poddles did them, dragging me after her.

But the squirrels were hibernating or something of the sort; or maybe they had seen Poddles afar off. They were not there; not the twitch of the grey tail of a one did we see. And Poddles wept on to the already damp grass. I had promised her squirrels, she said, and squirrels she would have or she would hold her breath and stamp her feet. More high spirits!

But presently she forgot that for a while. She was "firsty," and we hastened to the road again, where she ran me up a bill of threepence.

In the homeward tram, Poddles quickly gained the attention of seven or eight people, to whom she spoke thus, several times:

"We've been to Kew Gardens to see the squirls, and we didn't see them, and this is my uncle and he couldn't find the squirls, and my dad would have found lots of squirls, and this is my uncle and he had a drink out of my glass 'cause he was firsty too."

Later I told Poddles' father a little about it all.

"Oh, that's nothing!" he said. "Nothing to what she can do! I wonder if she's sickening for anything."

The Mayflower

I knew there were flowers in the long box before I opened it; the postmark and the handwriting told me that; and as I stripped off the outer wrappers there came to my nostrils that sweet smell of damp earth that makes one hunger so. The length of the package was unusual. A cardboard collar-box or a folding soap carton will suffice for primroses, violets, or wood anemones; but this was ten inches long.

It held a spray of hawthorn, and the scent of a deep-cut lane in May-time. The topmost of the delicate green buds had already released their frail white stars.

"This is the first of it," said the note; "you won't get it in London for a week or two yet. Down here everything is dancing." (But why rub it in? thought I.)

Beneath the hawthorn lay two roots of the wood violet ("you may be able to acclimatise these, but if they're wise, they'll die," said the note), and wriggling between the crumbs of earth a bright yellow "hundred legs."

I planted the violets in the shade of the fence, and tipped the "hundred legs" on to the mould, with a vague idea in my mind that he slays and eats the predatory green fly.

The spray of hawthorn I placed in a vase of Wedgwood blue, and it became a thing to worship. It lit the room and made me sing. All sorts of foolish songs I sang, including "Sumer is i-cumen in" to a wondrous air of my own devising, and "The cows are in the clover"; as well as a lot of other ditties having no reference to the matter in hand. But a fine morning and a delicate spray of hawthorn will turn the most prosaic ratepayer into an harmonious lunatic, or should do.

With me the world was just beginning; and I went round the garden five times to the cleaning of one boot, and barked at the dog next door, who barked back, and sang a little song to the tulips. Looking at it from this distance, I begin to think it was all a little foolish; but there it is.

Mrs. Boddy spoilt it. She is a commonplace person without an atom of poetry in her make up. She spends her life paddling with her knotted hands and arms in other people's soapsuds, for two shillings a day and threepence in lieu of beer. Her business is to fill my rooms with steam and the odour of soap, to rattle pails together, and to say regularly, washing-day after washing-day, "Well, whoever washed these 'ere things last ought to wash one more and then drop dead, they did, so there!"

My only complaint against Mrs. Boddy is that she sits on me so.

"You are 'ard on your socks," she says. "Ought, by rights, to 'ave more. Why, one young gennelman as I does for 'as as many as fourteen pair, all goin' at once, 'e does, so there!" I am always apologising for my wardrobe.

Another thing about Mrs. Boddy is her bonnet. It is built of black crêpe, with a suggestion of dust about its folds, and it rises from her brow to a great height, capped by a nodding geranium. And I think she never takes it off. Sometimes I have peeped round the door to see her without it, but her head is hidden in the mist from the tub; only her decapitated trunk appears, labouring from side to side. But in that fog I know her bonnet is nodding.

The dingy grey of its dusty folds merges into the grey dinginess of her hair. There is no dividing line, no fixed horizon where one can say, "Here ends Mrs. Boddy, and here begins the bonnet."

There is an ever-present sense of greyness about Mrs. Boddy; she seems to have no object in life but soapsuds, and the only thing I have ever seen her smile at is a line full of clean clothes. So I took her in to see the blue vase and its hawthorn spray. Mrs. Boddy wrinkled and twitched her little nose, like a rabbit with a lettuce leaf.

"Nesty stuff," she said. "Bring you no end of bad luck, that will. May! That's what it is. Knew it soon's I set eyes on it. Used to get it from Eppin' when a kid, but my mother wouldn't never 'ave it nigh

97

the place. Nesty stuff, and unlucky, too, if all they says be true. Accidents, I've 'eard of; children gettin' runned over with it in their 'ands. Nesty stuff!"

"But isn't it beautiful!" I protested. "Look at the little pinky-white buds, like fat babies. It's spring, Mrs. Boddy. Spring, and you ought to be dancing, so. Doesn't it all mean anything to you, Mrs. Boddy?"

"It's the blood," said the lady. "At this time of the year it is liable for to get rampageous. Now, my poor, dear mother used to get a pound of senna pods—there was nine of us—and a pound of salts—"

And so she went on, all the while peeling imaginary soapsuds from her arms, and slapping them into an imaginary bath.

There are a lot of Mrs. Boddys in the world. A day or two ago I travelled in a railway carriage with a young lady and her husband. A patch of flaming tulips caught his eye, and "Did you think to get the soft soap for the roses?" he asked.

"Yes, dear," said the lady, "and your face is all coming out in spots again." There is a subtle connection if you search for it.

"It's bad luck, too," went on Mrs. Boddy; "same's them liddle red flies with the black spots, them what-d'-you-call-'ems, you know."

"Ladybirds," I said; "dear little ladybirds. Isn't there a tragic song about one of them?

Ladybird, ladybird, fly away home,
Your house is on fire, your children are gone!

How does it go?"
Said Mrs. Boddy:

"All except one, sir, and her name is Fan, sir,
And she crept under the pudden-pan, sir.

That's what I used to sing as a gal. Parcel of silly nonsense."

Poor Mrs. Boddy! After a long and damp life, to have to do other people's washing, to have to listen to me drivelling. No wonder the steam has entered her soul. There is small room for frivolity at two shillings a day and threepence in lieu of beer. She would not be cheered up.

"Look at the sky," I said; "look at the blue of it, and look at that spray of hawthorn."

"Paper says rain," answered Mrs. Boddy; "an' you'll have an accident sure's you're alive if you keep that there May in the 'ouse. Nesty stuff!" And she gave me more evidence. Her niece's little boy, not the freckled one, but the one with the red hair; he brought home some May, and fell down the cellar steps and cut his lip open.

"And some coal dust got in, and so he had the mumps," concluded Mrs. Boddy.

It always happens like that. I get up and sing in my bath, and dance downstairs, and pipe like a thrush in mating time. Then comes Mrs. Boddy to dull my rose-coloured spectacles with her everlasting steam.

"Then there was young Bert Moneypenny," she continues. " 'E was comin' 'ome on 'is bike with a lot of it, an' in King-street, 'Emmersmif 'e—"

"Go away!" I shouted. "Go and sob in the copper! Go and be miserable somewhere else, and good morning, Mrs. Boddy."

"I'm sure, sir, I 'opes you'll get 'ome safe; but with that button-'ole—" And I have been filling in the blank all the week.

The Beacon Fire

The benighted traveller, says someone (Stevenson, I think), should always make his way down hill to lower ground. Thus he will come in due time to the sound of running water. Towards this he should steer his course, and so, by following the flow of the stream, he will assuredly come to the haunts of men once more. Better still if he see afar off the kindly glow of a light, for there he will find warmth and fellow-humans, and, maybe, food and drink.

Therefore my heart sang within me when, at the end of a road that I knew not, in a suburb where I was an alien, I saw the lively warmth of a distant fire. It was not a night watchman, standing sentry over a hole in the road, for his fire stands in a brazier, or is contained in a perforated pail; while this remote light was rectangular in shape. From time to time small red-hot coals, drops of fire, fell from it to the damp roadway, dulled, and went out.

As I drew near, the man who tended this strange fire rattled his fire irons and poked away at his strange furnace. And as he stoked he chanted a dolorous chant in a dolorous minor key.

"All 'ot, all 'ot!" was the burden of his dirge. A baked potato merchant!

This then was what my heart had leaped at. An Italian with a knowledge of English beginning and ending with "All 'ot." All up and down that street, with its chill houses, sightless windows, and closed doors, I had no friend; no one to put me on my road, or lend me a match; and my Italian vocabulary was made up entirely of such things as *Corpo di Bacco* and *Il Trovatore*.

But the fire drew me, and at the sound of my footsteps, the man with the poker moaned, "All 'ot!" I stopped beside him, and though the shaft of light from the bottom of his stove did not reach his face, I knew what was hid there in the blackness. A swarthy skin, brass earrings, black, oiled hair, and a red neckerchief. But even as I speculated a little glowing coal burst like an asteroid from the heart of the fire and lighted on his hand. He said something rapidly, and immediately I knew him for an Englishman.

It was a warm, moist evening, and the last thing I wanted was a hot potato. But I bought one anyway.

If you have never eaten a baked potato at 11 p.m. in a suburban street, get you out and do so at once. For it is an adventure; nay, it is an art worth the cultivating.

First you take the potato in your left hand and pass it quickly into your right; now roll it back to the left again, stamp your feet once or twice, trundle it over to the right once more, and put the fingers of your left hand into your mouth until you want them again. From one hand to the other, and back again, you pass the potato, blowing with your lips the while. You may have seen professional jugglers doing something like this with oranges.

The dainty prepared, it must now be eaten fragment by fragment from the point of a penknife. And as each piece rests on your tongue the correct thing is to draw in your breath sharply through pursed lips. Why, I do not know; but it is so.

The best baked potatoes are undoubtedly those one bakes oneself, in the embers of the oast-house fire in hop-roasting time. Then, of course, the first piece of the vegetable is thrown saltless out of doors, that the Little People may be appeased; but all the fairies have left town years and years ago. So I dug at mine with my penknife and fell to thinking about baked potato men in general and the one beside me in particular.

As he moved slowly across and across the front of his fireplace, feeding the heat from a bag of coke in the gutter, the beam of light showed me his face once or twice; and I noticed that he had whiskers. At first in the shifting half-light I took them for a grey muffler, but presently I recognised them as being of the variety known as the Newgate Fringe. They grew beneath his chin, from ear to ear, like an

Elizabethan ruffle. Their unlovely name is derived from the fact that they are supposed to interfere with the hangman's duties.

"Baked potato man," I said, "what are you doing out here to-night? It is fifty something in the shade, the apple trees are out, and I am wearing my thin underclothes. The season of the baked potato is past; sing hey! for the hokey-pokey."

"Lummy!" he answered, and stared. "Lummy! but I thought you was sober."

After some little discussion, I convinced him that his first thoughts were the kindest as well as being the truest, and we resumed the conversation on slightly less rhapsodic lines.

"Tell me," I pursued, "what do you do throughout the summer? No man with whiskers ever sold ice-cream. Where do you hide your can? Where do you hide yourself? Do you, tortoise-like, hibernate, or assume the chrysalid form? Do you curl up like a dormouse in winter and sleep till the baked potatoes come out again?"

Opening the bottom drawer of his outfit, he pinched and prodded one or two of his wares, turned some, and transferred a select few to the top shelf.

"Them's done," he said. "I've cooked more 'n I shall sell to-night. These 'ere summers, they'll be the ruin of us before long. The 'eat waves and the Italians between 'em; they'll do us in, they will."

Followed a comprehensive dissertation on Italy, her natives and their ultimate fate. He was a doleful person.

"Taters is goin' out," he said. "People don't like to be seen eatin' 'em in the street like they used to. Only drunks. Why, I've known real toffs fill their pockets with 'em in the cold weather, just to keep their selves warm, I 'ave. But now—I'm goin' to chuck it, I am. A ruined industry, that's what it is, ruined. We don't git them good old-fashioned winters now, we don't. Why, I've known nights as I've 'ad a reg'lar crowd round me. Couldn't serve 'em fast enough; an' to-night I've sold five penn'orth. 'Ave another, cocky, for old time's sake."

"But, tell me, baked potato man," I said, "what do you do in the summer?"

"I'm a sailor," he said, and I jumped.

"Yus," he continued; "I'm a sailor—on a water-cart." And he laughed a doleful laugh. "The borough council 'll soon be sending for me," he continued, "so I shan't put any fresh taters in. If we get another cold snap I shall 'ot these up, an' go on 'ottin' 'em up till they're gone. Then I shall pawn the old can an' the coke and the salt and vinegar wot's over, and go for a sailor. You see, mister, on this job I don't git me proper rest. If I nods, I falls on the oven; but with a 'orse as knows the neighbourhood, you can go right off to sleep on a water-cart. 'Ave another tater?"

I declined, lit my pipe at his fire, and asked my way.

"Elephant? Five minutes' walk. Round there, and round there again, and—but you're sure to get lost. I'll come with you if you're goin' to the Elephant. I'm as dry as a lime kiln, I am. Nobody won't pinch my old can … Tram? Won't 'ave time to stop? Oh, well, p'raps it wouldn't be safe to leave my pitch. Ask a copper. 'E'll tell you."

The Story-Teller

I am looking for a fat man with a red throat, an agile Adam's Apple, a bass voice, and yellow boots. Not any man with these qualifications, but one in particular. He wears a very low collar, and for a fat man his neck is long.

You have seen those celluloid balls that are poised on jets of water in shooting galleries. They bob up and down; now rising, now falling; now up again, now down once more. That is what this man's Adam's Apple does as he talks. Once it went so low I thought he had swallowed it, but it rose again. You will know him by this, and if you see him, avoid him as you would the Evil One, shun him as you would shun the plague; or stick to him like a leech, follow him home, and force your way into his house if necessary.

I will be more explicit.

This man and another got in an Underground train on Wednesday night last at Mansion House station. The second man does not matter; he was only a super. They sat facing me, and at once the silence of the carriage was broken by the fat man. In a deep voice he said, without any prelude or warning:

"Soon as I opened the gate the Chinaman nipped out of the rhododendrons, nipped over the fence, and scooted like billy-oh."

A staid-looking man in the corner dropped his paper and cocked his ear. The fat man proceeded:

"Minnie let me in, and the first thing she says was, 'Have you found the aspidistra?' I hadn't seen no aspidistra, and said so. Course, she started grizzling; so I said, 'Here, you stop that, and run upstairs and fetch the dagger off the bed.' "

Two other men stopped reading, and turned their eyes to the advertisements on the roof of the car. The man next to me leaned forward a little. The fat man's larynx climbed and fell and climbed up under his chin again, and his neck became more red than ever.

"She went upstairs, and presently I heard her yell like fits; and down she came again, falling over the stairs two at a time. 'The dagger's gone,' she hollered … What's this? Oh, Charing Cross! I was down here last night seeing young Alf off to Folkestone. That's Jim's boy, you know; the second, next to young George. He's got a good job down in Folkestone, with his uncle."

The man next to me shuffled his feet impatiently. In the corner the staid man was tearing at his thumbnails, while his neighbour's lips moved in wicked words.

The super to whom the fat man addressed himself came to our rescue.

"Minnie," he said; "what about Minnie and the dagger?"

"Oh, that!" said the Adam's Apple. "Well, she came scampering downstairs, and I could see that something was up. 'The dagger's gone,' she says, 'and little Ronnie's photo off the chest of drawers, and Amy's hair.'

" 'That's rum,' I said. Course, you could understand the photo going, because naturally they'd want that, but I couldn't see what use Amy's hair was going to be to them. That's Amy that used to be in the Stores, you know. So her hair don't come into it at all. 'That's queer,' I said … St. James' Park. I'm going on to Hammersmith. You get out at Earl's Court, don't you?"

The conductor came right into the carriage, opened a window, and banged it again noisily. I think we were all grateful to him. The fat man leisurely filled his pipe as the train ran into Victoria. Folding his paper slowly, the man in the corner collected his bag and umbrella, and got up. He glanced sorrowfully, almost imploringly, at the fat man, and turned to go. The larynx started to fluctuate again.

"What was I talking about? Oh, yes, of course. Well, as I say, I could understand the dagger being gone"—the staid man sat down again as if he had made a mistake—"but Amy's hair I couldn't get over. How they found it I don't know, but found it they had, and it was gone. Young Min was in a frightful way about it. What with that and the aspidistra, she was fair worked up. I went and had a look at the bedroom, and it was all turned topsy-turvy, but not a thing had they touched but that photo and that hair. 'That's funny,' I said, 'very funny.' Gloucester Road, isn't it? You get out at the next, don't you?"

"I'm going on to Hammersmith to-night," said his companion. "Got to see a man." We were all going on to Hammersmith. You could see that. Some of us were praying for a breakdown, an hour in a tunnel. For my part I was most interested in the Chinaman. I wanted him to come on again, and explain himself. What was he doing in the rhododendrons? It was most inconsiderate of the man with the pump-handle larynx.

" 'Nother queer thing we noticed," he continued presently, and even the train seemed to be holding its breath and listening.

"On the doorstep somebody had dropped a bottle of ink. Hadn't half made a mess. Oh, yes, and in the rhododendrons I found a cigarette picture. I believe I've got it here. No. Wait a minute, p'raps it's here. No … Course, silly, I gave it to young Ernie. He's collecting 'em. Got over a hundred and fifty, I believe." My neighbour drew a long breath and clenched his fist.

"So I took that and the bits of ink bottle round to the station, and they sent a plain-clothes man back with me.

"He goes into it all properly, and presently he points out a spot of blood on the handle of the gate. Baron's Court, this one. He did some measuring, an' then went up to the bedroom. First thing he saw was something I hadn't noticed. That's the best of having a trained mind on a thing. They learn to think along different lines to ordinary people, you know."

It was very oppressive in the train as we neared Hammersmith. The fat man yawned elaborately, searched all his pockets for his ticket, and lit his pipe again.

We were very near now, running in almost. The fat man stood up and caught a strap. His friend stood up, too; we all stood up. We would follow him in a body.

"He saw it," said the fat man, "but I missed it. Somebody had been writing across the mirror with a bit of soap. Same's they do on the cookshop windows, you know. To-day's menu. Let's see, now what was it?" The train slowed down, stopped, the doors opened, the fat man stepped along the carriage, and the man next to me stifled a shriek.

"Let's see, something about—no, that wasn't it. Oh, I know! It said—" and the door crashed behind him.

I got up to give chase, but the train was already on the move. As we passed him I caught a last glimpse of his larynx. It was on the up road. When I sat down the four or five people he had left behind were using their handkerchiefs on their foreheads.

You realise my desire to find the brute. I have tried to build up the beginning and end of the story, but it cannot be done. Frankly, I don't believe a word of it. I think he just goes round in trains telling this fragment to drive people mad. So if you hear a fat man, with an agile Adam's Apple, start a story about a Chinaman, an aspidistra, and Amy's hair, get it all by some means or other. Or, better still, run away.

But if you do get the story, let me know what was on the looking-glass.

The Shepherdess

In defiance of the regulations, which nagged at me like a maiden aunt from the wall of the carriage, I lay down at full length on the hot plush cushions and thought to sleep. A newspaper placed under my boots made me feel astonishingly virtuous; and in five minutes, lulled by the steady plug-plug of the train (there was a flat place on one of the wheels, I think), I began to doze.

At the very next stop the carriage door opened, and a woman's voice said:

"Go quietly, me dears, and don't wake the gen'leman. He's got five tickets all to 'isself." What could I do but sit up after she had put it so delicately?

She was a grey old lady, with a twinkling eye and she wore a stuffy-looking cape covered with black beads that rattled as she moved, and a huge white apron. Behind her trooped what I took to be a Sunday school. One by one she picked them up and threw them into the carriage, checking them off as she did so.

"Come on, young Milly; in you go. An' young Alfie, an' young Ernie, an' young Kitty, an' young 'Erbie. Oop-se-daisy!"

She settled herself in the corner, and beamed, then mopped her face on a corner of the apron.

"Sorry to disturb you, young feller," she said; "but if I don't git this little lot 'ome to-night, my boy won't 'arf crack on. They're 'is, you see, an' I'm a-takin' 'em out for the day. 'Alf a dozen of 'em, an' a tidy 'andful, too. If I was to lose one, 'e'd be cross as anythink. 'Arf a dozen of 'em. There's young Ernie, an' young 'Erbie, an' young Milly, an' young Kitty, an' young Alfie, an' ... 'ere, 'alf-a-mo, cocky! There's young Ernie, that's one, an' young Erbie two, an' young Milly three … Law, bless me 'eart an' soul, what a start I give meself. Couldn't only make five of 'em, an' 'ere I am a-nursin' young Artie. Oo! de picky lil sing, den. Did 'is ole gran'mo'er forget 'im den, did she?"

Young Artie took not the slightest notice, except to blow one or two bubbles. His silence seemed to annoy the old lady, so she turned him upside down, hit him in the back with her clenched fist, pulled some of his clothes up and some of them down, and laid him across her knees. And all the time she crooned and mothered him, saying with that twinkle in her eye: " 'E's a picky lil dee-yar, yes, 'e was. A booful boy, yes, 'e was."

While I would not have gone so far as that in my enthusiasm for the physical beauties of the baby, I was prepared to admit that it was a quiet child, strangely quiet. But then I am an amateur, and while a silent baby suggests that all is not well, a squalling infant makes me think of those long pins that mothers jab so casually into their offspring.

Young Artie continued to blow bubbles, and to gaze in wide-eyed surprise at his nurse. For grandmother clucked like a hen, and neighed like a horse, and jerked her head backwards and forwards, and rubbed her face against the baby's and cooed, and tumbled the child over and under and up and down, and hit it in the stomach, and walloped it in the back, until I expected to see young Artie come apart. But he just pouted and blew bubbles.

Then there was a fight in the other corner of the compartment. Young 'Erb had rubbed his boots against Milly's white frock. Young Alfie had taken Milly's part, and Kitty had ranged herself alongside young 'Erb; and the two sides were pulling hair. So grandmother tongue-lashed the lot of them, and I threw my newspaper under the seat.

"You, young 'Erb, you just be'ave yourself, else I'll take you in 'and, an' then you'll know it. You keep your feet down off the cushings, d'you 'ear? You, Minnie, where's your 'ankercher? What's the good of you 'avin' a clean 'ankercher if you don't use it? You're more trouble than you're worth, the lot of you. All except young Artie.

'E knows 'ow to be'ave, don't 'e, then? The picky lil toffee drop, 'e is."

She threw the baby affectionately to the roof once or twice, spun it round and round a little, and bit its chin. This time young Artie protested. His top lip lifted a little, the bottom one trembled, the bubbles stopped. Slowly his mouth lengthened, drooping at the corners, then widened, showing his pink and toothless gums; wider yet, till the roof of his mouth lay bare. Then the yell!

Harder and harder granny worked, pitching and tossing the infant from one arm to the other, rolling him on to his stomach, and patting his back while she danced her knees about.

"There, did 'is ole granny frighten him, did she, then? Never mind, ducky, den, an' if you don't stop that snifflin', young Milly, I'll 'alf kill you, I will." I don't think she meant that, but there was certainly extreme provocation. The carriage was full of it.

"Naughty ole granny, she was, den. Ssh! … My gracious, what a mouth! What a trap! Never mind, den.

Lavender's blue, diddle diddle,
Lavender's green.

Are you goin' to stop that snifflin', young Milly?

When I am king, diddle diddle,
You shall be queen.

Ain't there enough row with 'im without you 'owlin' away there, all the lot of you? 'Ow do you think the gen'leman can read 'is paper? I'll see your father further before I take you all out again … Bless 'is lil 'eart, it's the nasty toosums what's worryin' 'im, it is. The nasty ole toosey pegs.

Johnny Morgin played the orgin,
Kitty played the drum;
Mother played the tambourine,
An' Sally went pom-pom-pom!

Ain't it all right, young man, eh? 'Ark at 'im! Just 'ark at 'im. Nothink wrong with 'is chest, is there? But 'is father was jes' the same. Didn't git no sleep with 'im for two years, when 'e was gittin 'is teeth ... If I come over there to you, young 'Erb, I'll knock your 'ead off, I will, so there ... A little imp, that one ... There, there, my pet, diddums. Oh, crumbs! I do wish 'e'd shut up, the lil ducky, den, 'e was ... My pore ole 'ead, ain't 'alf agoin' fourteen to the dozen, an' I couldn't 'alf do a cup o' tea ... 'Ere's our station ... Let me go first, d'you 'ear? ... Now then, come on young Ernie, an' young 'Erb, an' young Milly, an' young Alfie, an' young Kitty. Oop-se-daisy! One, two, three, four, five, an' I've got one, that's six ... Good-night, young feller."

The Lions

The literature provided by the management of the Pike and Anchor is not extensive. There is a Farrier's Almanack for 1865, with a complete list of horse fairs and hirings, and a page of recipes for saddle galls; a Popular Educator of '74 (vol. 3, Bac. to Bug.), and a "Pilgrim's Progress." Farcy buds and saddle galls are not hot weather entertainment, and the article on Backgammon was dull reading, too. Bunyan is better, but my favourite chapter, containing the fight between Christian and Apollyon, is missing.

Once upon a time that was one of my favourite fights, sharing a big corner of my heart with two other immortal "scraps," the duel in the rigging of the *Hispaniola*, in "Treasure Island," and Brown v. Slogger Williams.

There was a stricken apple tree in the old garden that served for the *Hispaniola*, and terrible scenes might have been witnessed there. "One step further up that ladder, Mr. Hands, and you're a dead man." We were not word-perfect, but I think we improved on Stevenson a little. We were sure he would not have minded.

"The Pilgrim's Progress" without the fight is a book for the cloister rather than for the back garden of the Pike and Anchor. So for an hour I have sat and gazed through half-shut eyes at the green bay. White regiments of tumbling wave-tops are marching up the sands in right form of war; and above, one poised gull breaks the deep blue. In the garden at my feet the roses are bursting their green shells and great brown bees swim over the clumps of thrift. Work is difficult.

At eight o'clock this morning a ship went past the bay about ten miles out. Just a something on the skyline with a mile-long black smudge trailing behind it. So seldom do they come in as near as this that the village turned out to do the honours; twenty or thirty of us at the water's edge, telling one another who she was and where she was bound. Old Trewynhale, who is blind and could not see her, waved a handkerchief, and told us of a craft that came ashore here in the winter of sixty something. A collier she was, and the village bought no fuel for six months. "There was a boy drowned, an' I got 'bout five hundredweight of coal an' no end of wood and rope and stuff, besides a fine brass can'lestick." But the story only lasted until ten o'clock, and then I came back to the garden.

Halfway down the cliff the management of the Pike and Anchor is digging potatoes; it is fine to lie and look at him. As he digs he sings:

Oh, the birds were a-singing in the mo-orrning,
The ivy and the myrtle were in bloom;
The sun on the hills was a-dawning,
And that's where I laid her in the tomb. Ta-ra-ra!

He is a merry soul, and his song is the current melody here. Has it reached you yet? The last line, I think, does not appear in the original; but as it is sung it seems to come straight from the heart of the singer.

From the house comes the clatter of dishes where Miriam washes up. She is the management's daughter, two plaits, bare legs, and fourteen summers old. When I clap my hands thrice she comes to me carrying a brown mug with blue bands, brimming with cider. There is no doubt that here, at least, all's right with the world. Our days are fourteen hours long, each hour a day; if it were not for the going and coming of the sun, time would not exist. There are no posts.

We have just received news of your hailstorm of Tuesday. A few of us believe it, but even these are shaken when they look at the sky. "Impossible!" we say, touching wood.

This morning Miriam came to me as I lay in the garden, and "Don't you find it dull?" said she.

"Frightfully," I answered. "I wish I were back at work, back in London sitting in the breeze from the motor-buses, inhaling the invigorating vapours from hot tar paving." She hardly knew what to make of this.

"Must be dull here after London," she said, and went back for more cider as compensation. Presently a bright idea struck her, and she came down the garden again.

"Tell you what," she said. "You've never been here before, have you? Well, I'll tell you what I'll do. After I've washed up each evening, if you like, I'll go for a walk with you, and show you the—the places of interest." She was quite excited about it, and kept tying and untying her plaits beneath her chin as she talked.

"It isn't so dull really," she continued; "not when you know your way about. There's quite a lot of interesting places about—and stories, and all that, you know."

"You can tell me the stories now, if you like," I said, "while I go to sleep. That'll save time." But Miriam had laid herself out to cheer me up, and would not be deterred.

"We could go down Dead Man's Lane to-night," she said. "It's a little narrow lane right away from everywhere, and a long time ago they found a man there dead. And now nobody won't go up there after dark, 'cos they DO say—"

"Never mind about that one," I said. "I seem to know it. Tell me about the Devil's Chimney Pot."

"How did you know there was a Devil's Chimney Pot?" asked Miriam.

"There always is," I replied; "just as there's always a Dead Man's Lane and a Cut Throat Corner."

"You've been here before," said Miriam reproachfully.

"Never," I said; "but it's as if I saw it all. So if you don't mind, we'll miss those. And I don't think there's any need to see the Lover's Leap either, nor the Devil's Punch Bowl. In fact, we might altogether ignore the landed estates of His Satanic Majesty." Miriam's face was getting longer and longer.

"But round the Point," she said, "there's the Devil's Kitchen, a big cave with no bottom to it, and they DO say—"

"Let them say," I protested. "We know the story, and I could make up a better one myself. The same applies to the Seven Sisters and the Two Brothers and the Man and His Dog and the Lover's Seat and the Lion and Lamb." Miriam was cross now.

"Clever, aren't you?" she said, pouting. "But there isn't a Lion and Lamb, and there isn't a Man and His Dog."

"What!" I exclaimed. "Not two rocks close together, where a man was drowned whose dog can be heard barking above the roar of the waves on the darkest night as the clock strikes twelve?"

"There's two rocks," admitted Miriam, "and they're close together, but they're called the Cow and Calf, and they DO say—"

"More cider, Miriam," I said, "and let there be a head on it. Now that I know the local legends are intact, I would sleep."

"I thought it'd be dull for you," remonstrated Miriam, "but you're making it worse."

"Much better," I said. "For instance, do you know the story of the 'Mermaid in the Brown Tweed Skirt'? It's frightfully exciting, and it took place in that dark pool behind the Pulpit Rock."

"Is it a real story?" asked Miriam. "There is a Pulpit Rock, but you haven't seen it, so how do you know? You only came yesterday, and you've been asleep ever since."

"When you grow older, child," I said, "you will know that there is always a Pulpit Rock, just as there is always a Cut Throat Lane. For the story, if you will come back in an hour with a mug of cider, I'll have it ready for you."

Ambition

Given a fine morning, breakfast is usually laid to the "Ballade of Lord Bateman," with "Hold the Fort" on Sundays and holidays. As I climb the steep garden path, I hear the opening couplet sung in jerks, thus:

"Lord Bateman was—a noble man,
A noble man—of high degree."

That is Miriam with the cloth and spoon basket going from the kitchen to the parlour. As the song draws to its end, I go indoors and take my seat.

"He kissed her wunst,—he kissed her twice,
And on his neck—full sore sobbed she.

You mustn't be in such a hurry. If you don't give it time to draw, 'twill be nothing but water bewitched." After that comes the news of the household, items of kitchen gossip that help a meal wonderfully.

"Our old Tiddles-Puss have gone off three days now, and no sight or sound of her. Poachin', I reckon. And the Plymouth have killed three of her chicks, so father have given the rest to Brown Betty. That makes her 14 in family. Don't think she'll be able to cover 'em, do you?" I think not, knowing nothing whatever about it.

"Got one of my plaits in the cream 's'morning," she goes on. "Going to tread on strange ground, I expect. Wonder where that'll be." Thus do we chatter the meal away, for to-day's paper will not arrive until the day after to-morrow; and before I get it the postman has got to

116

slip it from the wrapper and digest the headlines for later use in the Young Men's Institute.

A morning or two ago there was no "Lord Bateman," so that I was late for breakfast. All through that meal Miriam did not appear, and when she came to clear away she brought a cold wind with her, a sense of gloom. Perhaps the picture framed by the window had something to do with it, for the bay was hid in crawling fog, and the further cliff could not be seen. A sun about as brilliant as a pearl shirt button tried to get through, but was beaten; and in an hour everything was dripping moisture.

"Got out of bed wrong side, I think," said Miriam. "Everything's rotten 's'morning, and I've got the hump."

Now, hump may come from liver or digestion or bad luck, from a score of things, but it should never come when it is June, and one is fourteen. I explained all this.

"I'm forty 's'morning," said Miriam, and for a long time I could get no more than that.

"Don't you reckon this is a dull old hole?" she asked presently. "Nothing to see, and nothing to do, and nothing to hear. Same old sea, same things to look at every morning. Never meet nobody or see nobody ... Well, there's you; but you're a visitor. Better'n some, p'raps, but you're a visitor, and by rights I didn't ought to be a-sitting here talking to you."

She twisted her plaits beneath her chin and rubbed the calf of her right leg up and down the shin of her left, a sure sign of impatience. Then suddenly:

"Susie Polgate came home last night. She've been up to a place in London, in service, and she've been telling me all about it." (So it was not the mist over the bay.) "She'm maid in a great big house with ten other maids, and she gets Fourteen Pounds a year and tips, and one print frock and one black dress length, and all found. She'm coming up here 's'evening to tell me some more. You ought to see her. Short skirts and coloured stockings and shoes with heels on 'em. And she knows all the songs and sayings, and she's been to theatres and those moving picture things." (It was pouring out now, in a flood.) "And she gets one evening a week and one whole day a month, and goes to hear the band in the Park, and she's got a young man."

A nice problem to tackle on a holiday; a girl, brought up on a cliffside overlooking a blue bay, where the coldest wind that blows is a mild south-wester, and primroses and violets bloom on Christmas day, pining for what is called "life," yearning for service in London and one evening a week. That was what I made of it, and soon it all came out. Susie had sown the seeds of that divine discontent all right.

"Better than moping here," she said in a little while. " 'S'pose I'll go on getting breakfast and cooking eggs and feeding chicks till I'm all twisty, like gran'mo'er, and too crotchety to live with. That's all you've got to do down here, live till ye die." What she said was true, but it is true of all of us. We live until we die, some differently from others, but only until we die. (I wish this sea-fog would clear.) But as you cannot talk like that to fourteen years, I put in a little lying. Tried to paint her life as she did not see it, to compare it with Susie's (whom, if I see, I shall smack). There was only neutral tint on the palette this morning, however, and the result was not brilliant.

"Of course you'll grow old and twisty," I said. "So will Susie. But if you stop here at the Pike and Anchor, you'll grow older and twistier than she will. Life in London, with one evening a week, is soon over. Why, I don't suppose for a moment that Susie's got her own little bedroom, with her own dressing-table like you have, and a little flower-box on the window-sill. She has to share hers with a girl she hardly knows.

"Now what you'll do is this," I went on. "You'll go on looking after your father, and feeding the chickens and making a fuss of Tiddles-Puss's kittens until you're about twenty-three. Then you'll marry young Bert Thatcher—"

"Shan't!" said Miriam, vehemently. "He bites his nails. If I marry anyone, it'll be young Saul Moneypenny."

"Then you and Mr. Moneypenny will take the Pike and Anchor over from your father, and let him dig the garden and feed the chicks till his time comes, and then … and then …"

"I've got as far as that myself before," said Miriam. "And then we'll wake up every morning, and go to bed every night for years and years and years. And then we'll all get twisty and crotchety like gran'mo'er, and that's all." I made one final effort.

"Long before that," I said, "Susie will be ready to give her one black dress length for a bunch of those sea daisies that Brown Betty's eating. You ask her in a year's time of it's all high heels and bands in the park." She looked out of the window for a space.

"Fog's going," she said. "You fishing 's'morning? Can I come?"

"If you'll promise to talk about something else," I said.

Next morning the bay was blue again, and we had "Lord Bateman" before breakfast.

The Omen

If you have youth enough not to be afraid of tombstones and their forlorn Hic Jacets, the wooden seat round the monkey-puzzler will provide full measure of entertainment.

The municipal authority, its fatherly eye on the living rather than the dead, has levelled the hillocks in the old burying-ground, and placed the worn stones against the walls. Where the grey-green memorials leaned awry is now neatly barbered turf with flaring geraniums.

For the relief of the local rates the path to the circular seat is of broken tombstones, with here and there the cheeks of a cherub still showing faintly. Names of men long dead still remain, the letters picked out with bright moss; Gents. for the most part, "Of this Parish." There were a-plenty of Esquires, too, in those days; and they spelled the title at length, scorning the brusque abbreviation.

The monkey-puzzler is part of these improvements, replacing a Cedar of Lebanon half as old as Time, which the parish surveyor and inspector of drains condemned as unsafe.

This was silly of the drain inspector, because an *araucaria* gives no shade worth the seeking, and the round seat is not comfortable until the sun has left it. Then I sit there sometimes, feeling first to see if the blistered green paint be sticky.

There is a hollow worn in the flagged path, and here, when the gardener has finished with the hose, the sparrows come to bathe and fight. I was watching their squabbles the other evening, and dreaming a wide-awake dream, when footsteps sounded on the stones, and the bathers fled away.

Two women came to the round seat; and one was stout, so that she puffed and blowed loudly, and the other was slim and easier of breath. My Spanish castles came toppling to earth (it was a beautifully ordered universe I was fashioning), for no man can day-dream in close proximity to a 12-stone woman dressed in a bonnet of nodding jet and a cape trimmed with bugles. Spring-side boots, too, are facts to slay fancies.

"I'm that thankful to sit down, my dear, you don't know!" That was the stout woman, with a wheezy intake of breath after each word. "I'm all of a fluster." She fanned herself with a handkerchief.

"Your legs is younger 'n mine," she gasped; "and you tear along like you was possessed. What with that an' the other trouble, I don't know whether I'm on my 'ead or my 'eels."

"You're on your 'eels," said her companion. " 'Ave a toffee?" A paper bag rustled.

" 'Ow you can sit there an' suck that stuff I can't think. In a graveyard, an' me at death's door for all I know. 'Tain't respectful."

"If I was you," said the thin woman, "I should 'ave polished elm an' brass 'andles. Lasts longer, I understand."

"You always was a scoffer," said the stout woman; "but you'll scoff once too often. You mark my words."

"Look at them spadgers, the little mucks," said the thin one. "Look at that little pot-'erb in the black shirt front. 'E ain't 'alf a scrapper, is 'e?" But the stout woman would not be comforted.

"I know my 'eart's weak," she puffed; "and I'm sure somethink 'll 'appen to me if somethink don't soon 'appen to me."

"You can tell me about it all over again, dear, if it'll ease you," said the thin woman soothingly.

"If I only knew what was in store," said the other, "I could resign myself to it. But to be everlastin' on tenter-hooks is that wearin', you don't know. It was the last of the dozen, too, an' for all I know that makes it worse." (I began to get excited.) "I left the supper things till this mornin' so as to do 'em all together with the breakfus' things," ("Patience, patience!" chirruped a listening sparrow) "because it ain't worth while 'ottin' water for only one lot, an' them not what you could call real dirty. Nothin' greasy, you know." (Yes, yes, madam, you were washing up, and—?) "I 'ad a bit o' cheese an' a ungyun; an' Liz, she finished up a round of German what was left over from the night before through young Alf not comin' 'ome to 'is supper."

"Saucy young 'ound," said the thin woman, jabbing at the bird's bath. "Don't want it all to yourself, do you? Go on, 'oppit, you!"

The story proceeded. "I no sooner took 'old of the thing, 'adn't even started to wipe it, before the rim come right off, a inch of it, right 'round, clean as a whistle, not a crack to be seen, an' it looks for all the world as if it 'ad been done a-purpose; and you wouldn't know but what it was meant to be like it." She took in a fresh supply of air and fanned herself again after this effort.

" 'Tain't the tumbler that I mind" ("Ah," said the listening sparrow), "though the 'ole dozen's gone now. It's what it means. An' I shook like a jelly for five minutes."

"It means that you'll 'ave to buy some new tumblers," said the thin woman, but the other swept along on the tide of her story.

"I didn't know *what* to do. If it's a thing like spillin' salt, you know where you are; or meetin' a cross-eyed man, or a 'orse with a white nose, or walkin' under a ladder.

"Black cats, too, I never was afraid of, an' shooshes 'em out of the 'ouse as soon as look at 'em. But tumblers I don't know nothink about. An' there ain't nothink about 'em in the dream book what come under the door last week, neither."

"You'll fright yourself into a early grave, that's what you'll do, my dear," said the thin woman. " 'Ave a toffee!"

"You may well laugh," said the other; "but one of these days you'll know all about it. Only a month ago I see the new moon over my right shoulder through glass. I spit on my finger an' made a cross on my left boot, but I knew it wasn't no good. Laid awake all night, I did, wonderin' what was goin' to 'appen to me. An' I wasn't 'alf glad when the chimbley caught fire two mornin's after! I knew what it was then.

"An' wasn't you with me when we met a load of 'ay? An' didn't I say somethink was goin' to 'appen to one of us? An' didn't you slosh a lump out of your 'and cuttin' bren butter a week after?"

"Them spadgers 'll catch their deaths, if they don't pop off 'ome," said the thin woman. " 'Ave a toffee? An if you're rested, we'll pop along."

"I ain't got the 'eart to sit and eat stick-jaw," said the stout one. "I shan't feel right till somethink's 'appened to me." She rose from the seat with a grunt, and prepared to go.

"Salt, an' two people sayin' the same thing at once, an' crossin' knives and boots on the table, I know all about. But I don't know nothink about tumblers."

"If it'd ease your mind," said the thin woman, as they walked down the path of epitaphs, "an' make you more comfortable, I'll shove you under a 'bus on the way 'ome."

And a sparrow who had found a worm hurrying across a "Here Lyeth" stopped in his meal to say, "Pip-pip."

The Snob

With a saint at the head of their profession, it is a little curious that menders of boots should be such aggressive and pugnacious persons. Every cobbler is, of course, something of a philosopher, and usually he is also a rebel, in thought if not in deed.

For instance, there was—let me see. There was—well, I cannot call to mind a good example just at present; but I can assure you it has always been so. Yet I cannot tell why I am so sure.

Curious how these ideas get into one's head, is it not? And when one has made an assertion such as the foregoing, it behoves one to do one's best to prove it.

To that end I have searched all the reference books at my immediate disposal, and but for two rather weak cases have come empty away. There was the bumptious cobbler who found fault with Apelle's picture, a little man, I should think, with his thumbs in the armholes of his waistcoat; and the naughty knave who leads the mob in the first scene of "Julius Caesar."

But I am certain there are heaps more somewhere, men like Wat Tyler and John Ball and Jack Cade.

I have looked under Boots and Shoes; under Cobbler and Snob, and even under such unlikely heads as Feet, and Brads, and Wax. There is a cursory mention of the poet, Hans Sachs, of Nuremberg, who, in the intervals of pot-hunting at local Eisteddfods, did a little soling and heeling; but from all accounts he was a peace-loving soul, and useless in support of my contention. Teufelsdröckh and Slawkenbergius, the only foreign authors with whom I am at all familiar, are silent on the point; and yet it seems as if they ought to have had something to say about it.

Maybe, the idea grew upon me out of my knowledge of Mr. Apps, who mends the village boots. He is a little man who sits all day in a little wooden hut opposite the horse trough, and he lives on brass tacks.

He wears big, circular spectacles, has a high forehead with a smear of heel-ball across it, and a chin that is always as prickly as the barrel of a musical box. His principal garment is a huge apron, with which at intervals he wipes his brow, polishes his spectacles, and dusts the tiny shop.

I like Mr. Apps, because, to use his own words, he "doesn't care the smell of an oil-rag whether he mends my boots or not." This attitude has one drawback; it makes Mr. Apps unpunctual, and usually I have to wait in the shop while he runs the hot welt iron round the blackened edges of my boots, and talks.

On the question of religious belief we have come to an understanding, but on everything else Mr. Apps is as dogmatic as a steam hammer, and drives each statement home with one smashing blow, as he drives home his pegs.

"I don't never believe in nothink what I can't see with my own eyes," he says; and, to stop further discussion, scoops up a huge handful of vicious-looking tacks, and hurls them down his throat. For a space he rolls these round and round with his cheeks distended, presumably to get all the points turned inwards; and he would, indeed, be an unfair antagonist who would attempt to argue with a man thus handicapped.

One by one he works the brads out between his lips, hammers them quickly into the upturned boot before him, and before the first lot is entirely disposed of a second handful is thrown down his gullet.

I have often wondered whether Mr. Apps has any check on his intake and output of tacks.

Sometimes, in moments of heat, he will try to talk while his mouth is thus distended, and the result is awe-inspiring to watch. At first his words come thickly through the mass of metal, his face gets red; and if he be very angry, his eyes will bulge, and the veins on his forehead swell.

The brads are holding him back, and if you want him to die, now is the time to mention rubber heels, or say something about the House of Lords being the bulwark of civil and religious liberty. If his hands were full, I think he would swallow the tacks rather than let the remark pass unchallenged.

As the tacks are used up his speech becomes gradually clearer, and at the end of each boot he flies to a tin can, which always stands on his stinking oil-stove.

As he stares at me over the rim of the vessel, I watch his larynx going up and down, until with a prolonged "A-a-ah!" he comes from behind the can, and wipes his lips on his apron.

"I wouldn't give no votes to no women, not if they was ever so," he says, and takes another dose of his favourite metal. Then mumbling through the impediment, "I gets 3s. 6d. for solin' and 'eelin' your boots, and only 2s. 9d. for a woman's."

"But that's because women have smaller feet," I ventured, "and do not require so much leather nor so many brads."

"Smaller feet!" says Mr. Apps. "Oh, 'ave they! Do they! Look at this little lot. Mrs. So-and-So, up the road. There's a pair of trotter-cases for you! There's plates-o'-meat! An' look at these! Mrs. What's-'er-name at the big 'ouse. There's daisy roots! There's a genteel 'oof for you. Smaller feet! I'll 'ave to make some more tea after that.

"Standin' 'ere, 'ammerin' away from early morn to doo-ey eve, makes you think," he told me. "The things I think of'd startle you out of your seven senses—five, I mean. Take this pair o' shoes I'm workin' on now. You can't see nothink in 'em but a pair o' shoes. Don't tell me, 'cos you can't, so there.

"But I can! There's all a man's character in those shoes. Look at the brown polish clogged in the brogues. Laziness! Look at the run-down 'eels. Meanness! Look at the broken laces tied in a knot. No self-respect! Look at the outside edge of the left sole. Bandy! Look at the way they're wore. Impe—what's-'is-name—cuniosity. Impecuniosity! He's a slacker, born tired, and an all-round dud, that's what 'e is."

"They're mine," I said.

Mr. Apps coughed and swallowed about a ha'porth of tacks.

The Gardener

Because he is in touch with every skipper who puts out of Rye Harbour, Old Man Wurzell receives at intervals huge consignments of "hard"; caked tobacco leaf that blunts one's knife like seasoned oak, but which is marvellous sweet in a pipe. And because his consumption is not what it was, he lets me have the residue in exchange for back numbers of the "Shipping Gazette" and any scraps of news from Lloyd's that may come his way.

With these he sits in his daughter's garden and smells the sea again, or talks of ships and men with whom he has worked. For Old Man Wurzell was a skipper of parts in his day and time; a lusty man with a reputation for getting things done. Then came his accident; a dark night, a hatch left off, a thirty-foot drop, and a drunken surgeon to set the leg.

So the old man went home slowly, on two sticks, to his married daughter in London; and now in winter time he sits by the stove and grows mustard and cress on a piece of damp flannel. His leg will not take him far. "Won't do a darned thing it's told," is his way of putting it; but now and again he hobbles to the bus for the City, and searches the shipping offices in Mark-lane and Billiter-street for cronies still at work; or passes the time of day with an old deck hand kicking his heels outside the Tower.

These days, he clings to the garden, stumping up and down the gravel paths with a strawberry punnet, collecting dead blooms, withered leaves, and weeds; and talking aloud to his flowers. The old sorts are his favourites. Love-in-a-mist, marigolds, sweet woodruff, honesty, heliotrope, bergamot, and the like.

"Now, my pretty dears," he says, as he toddles along the border, "what's amiss with you all this morning?" Then to a dahlia, its huge bloom heavy with last night's rain: "Eh, but I must lash you to a mast, else you'll fetch away and go overboard."

There are a couple of roses, too, that he tends as a mother her first baby.

"Sussex, they be! From my nephew down to Robertsbridge. Outlandish names they have, like a Dutch trawler, but beautiful creatures." He stoops over them, searching each leaf for the dangers I have told him of.

"Here, you great, fat rascal," to a caterpillar hiding below a leaf; "come you off, and take that!" But his fingers are "all thumbs," and have no knowledge of the strength of a caterpillar's hide.

"Made a mess of that one," he says. "But don't they know, the fat sluggards! Eating, eating, and doing nothing for their vittles. They woolley ones I don't mind so much, but the green and smooth ones I can't stand. And don't they know? Tell me they don't know! Always on the under-side, where no one can see 'em, and always the same green as the leaf. Don't they just know!"

I have tried to explain the theory of protective colouring to him, but he will have none of it. "You and your science stuff, and long names. They know, that's all. Don't they know!"

For green fly, who also know, he administers an evil brew of his pipe scrapings that is sudden death; and for their further torture, sits by his two roses and blows great clouds of heavy smoke through their branches.

"That'll make 'em cough their chests sore," he says, gleefully. "That'll teach 'em to come along here suckin' the blood of my roses that my nephew sent me from Robertsbridge. Cleaned yonder one last night with a brush, I did, and this morning it were covered again with the fat vermin. And some with wings! But this'll take the wind out o' their sails." And it would, indeed, be a sturdy aphid who could breathe Old Man Wurzell's tobacco smoke and live.

There is a little camp-stool that he lugs about with him from clump to clump of flowers, and on which he sits to do his overhauling.

Watch him before a bush of Canterbury bells, snipping off the dead blooms that they shall not seed and weaken the growth.

"Big families drag a man down," he says, "and so 'tis with flowers. Them as is done with is done with, and their going helps the rest to thrive.

"So come you off, you! You've done your trick, and now make way for your betters. And you, too! Ah! There's an earywig in that one. Come you out!" He probes into the cup with a spent match. "Come you out, you wriggly wig. Nasty things, they be, with ice-grabs in their tails. So!" There is an earwig the less in the world.

Bees he is mortally afraid of, but owns to a tremendous respect for their industry.

"Here you come again a-sailing," he says to a blundering golden busybody. "Hard at it, morning, noon, and afternoon. Bobbing in an' out and singing all the time ... Now then, you! Half a minute, half a blessed minute. I won't hurt ye! G'way, confound ye! I won't hurt ye. Sit down and rest a bit till all's done. No need to keep flustering about so. And you're wasting your time going in there, 'cos one big feller's just come out. All right, then. Have it your own silly way.

"I don't like 'em," he told me, "but I like they brown fellers better than they stripey ones. They do just tarrify me to death. Seems if they're coming after you, with a buzz like the wind through a guy. And what d'ye think of yonder bunch of what's-its-name, mignonette? Not a lot to look at, but her do smell so sweet.

"And now I'll give 'em all a tot of water, and let 'em go to bed."

So he spends each day, muttering among his posies, with the sea but a memory, until evening; when if it be warm he is allowed to sit in the garden for his last pipe. Then, deftly manoeuvring, I may lead him on to sing me "Spanish Ladies" or a polite version of the "Tinker of Amsterdam."

And now all this must come to an end. Old Man Wurzell's daughter's man must move. His cottage and garden are wanted for a railway, or a church, or something, and they are under notice.

" 'Tis to be," he said when he told me. "Sailing orders, and we leave in a month. Hetty's Jim, he be trying for a cottage near by, so's I can shift my flowers, but they're few and far spread. I've been looking myself this morning, and couldn't see a one. Lots of 'em, I s'pose, wouldn't stand shifting to new ground, eh? I thought so.

"But if I could take along my two roses from Robertsbridge, I wouldn't mind the others—not to speak of. Start afresh next spring, that's all. What houses I've seen have no sort of garden at all. Room for a dustbin, maybe, and a clothes-line.

"My girl, she says she reckons it'll have to be a flat. Mansions, don't they call 'em? Like cubby-holes with no backs at all." Then wistfully—

"I suppose I could have a couple of window boxes, eh?" Certainly I thought he might have window boxes, and with some flats there was a balcony. He hummed a little and sniffed at his mignonette.

Presently: "Roses'll grow in window boxes, won't they?"

Knowing different, I assured him that they would; and he stumped down the garden, singing—

"In Canton-street one summer's night,
   Hey-oh! Hey-ah!"

and came back with a nosegay for me.

The Flower Girl

It is not given to every man to see visions, more especially in the grey chill of early morning; but one came to me yesterday, on the Thames Embankment.

Close by the Temple Gardens the pavement was warmed by two great baskets of scarlet poppies and blue-grey lavender; warmed and sweetened, so that for a flash I thought myself elsewhere.

Behind the baskets stood a girl, full and fresh like the poppies. A large apron obscured most of her, and the rest of her dress, blouse, neckerchief, and hat, owed much to the primary colours, so far as I remember it. For her rich face drew the eye from all else; its fine oval, its deep brown eyes, and ripe, pouting mouth. A face that might have launched a thousand thousand ships.

She stood majestic, breathing hard, and swaying to straighten her back. One tanned forearm she drew across her forehead, and inspected the result.

But for her hat she might have been Ceres, ample and luxuriant, or Ruth, fresh from her gleaning, and I am afraid I stared; for she looked me up and down, and then, "Lummy! ain't it 'ot? Not 'alf, it ain't!" she said.

It was very early; only we and a few pigeons possessed the earth, and so I offered to carry one of the baskets for a space. A timid offer which I repented as I voiced it, an offer which in a broader daylight I would not have dared to make. To be chivalrous on the public highway at noon is to draw a crowd, and crowds giggle. But I need not have worried.

"Lift one of them there!" she said scornfully, and laughed so that the pigeons fled away. "Lift one of them there! You! No, cocky, it'd be cruelty to children. You'd come in 'alf, you would. You'd come unstuck." Again that full-chested merriment.

"Tell you what," she said, when her laughter had died away across the river. "Where you goin'—Temple?" Yes, I was going to the Temple station.

"Well, 'op in!" she said, and cleared a space among the poppies.

Soon after dawn these days, you will often find the East End side of Temple station ablaze with baskets of fresh summer blossoms, for this is the port whence the flowers from Covent Garden start their journey suburbwards.

There we presently arrived, I on my feet, for the suggestion that I should get into her basket and be carried was merely this person's idea of humour. She kept looking down at me, too, and laughed all the way.

A basket on each arm, and her ticket between her fine teeth, the girl walked past the ticket collector to the top of the stairs, took a firmer grip of her burdens, and went sideways down four steps. From the top came a penetrating voice—

Won't you buy—my bloomin' lavingder?
Fifteen big branches—for a penny!

She half turned, looked up, and continued her way, two more steps, and a rest. Only in the rests did she speak, so that her progress was thus punctuated:

"What's the—matter with—yer mouf?—muvver bin—feedin' yer—with a spade?"

At the bottom of the flight she put her baskets down and squared her shoulders; then shouted up the stairway: "Get some stitches put in that 'fore it tears, old son." There was no reply.

On the platform, seated on the handle of a basket of roses and early chrysanthemums, was a man, curly-haired and wearing earrings.

"Cheero, Meg!" he said, and "What, me old Jim," answered the girl.

We all got into the same carriage, and here I actually did help Meg with one of her baskets.

" 'Allo, Ronald," she said, by way of thanks, "you still 'ere?" Then to Jim, "Bin follerin' me about all the mornin', Ronald 'as. Tried to 'alf-inch my lavender once. 'E'll git on, 'e will."

She turned to him and filliped with the circlet in his ear.

" 'Ow's trade, old son?" she asked.

"Not so dusty," he said. "Young Art's gone on with the barrer. Runners is cheap and good, and so's marrers. Peas is right orf, rotten. Sprouts'll soon be in, and then Chris'mas. An' then, old trouble—" He slipped his arm behind the girl, caught her chin with the other hand, and pushed her head back. Then kissed her on her lips, noisily, once, twice, and again, all in the bright glare of the electric lights.

"Not in front of the children, old son," protested the girl. "Ronald's lookin'." I tried to read my newspaper.

"You don't 'alf look nutty 's'mornin'," said Jim presently. "Noo 'at, ain't it?" He looked her over slowly from head to foot.

"Old 'un done up," said Meg. "Only the ribbin's noo. Got it orf the girl in the shop what makes up the wreafs. Fine ribbin they 'ave, an' all goes to waste on the tombstones. Rolls an' rolls of it she'd got, white an' purple, some of it as wide as that. I says, 'Come on, ole dear! Take a inch orf the next two dozen fun'rals. They won't miss it,' I says. So she carves me orf 'alf a yard. Cost free bob in the shops, that would. Git some more 'fore Chris'mas, I will. White, next time."

They were silent for a space, wrapped in the future, no doubt; while Jim fashioned a cigarette.

"An' then no more hikin' them baskets about," he said. "Much as I can do."

"Don't you worry, cocky," said Meg. "I ain't bustin' to do no weight-liftin'. I'm agoin' to stand be'ind the stall an' 'oller an' take the dibs, an' sauce the coppers when they comes round for samples. Thievin' lot of 'oun's."

"Yes, an' get yer arms all chilblains as big as termarters. I'll watch it." He looked at her and laughed, jingled the money in his pockets, and stretched his legs across the carriage.

"You'll stop in the shop, you will," he said, "while I go round with the barrer." Evidently meant for a bombshell, this; but Meg was not moved.

"Oh, all right, Pierpont!" she said. "What did yer uncle die of?"

"It's a fact," said Jim. "A shop an' a moke, paid for an' all." The girl sat up and caught him by the jersey.

"You bin backin' 'orses?" she asked, fiercely.

"Go 'way, fat 'ead," said the man. Then seeing her concern, "Sold the round yes'day, and the stall an' pitch. Bought the shop corner of Church-street. Ole 'Oppy Isaac's shop. Now then, 'ow's that, umpire?"

The girl twisted her fingers together, then leapt at the man and kissed him shamelessly, out of the middle of which embrace I heard his muffled voice desiring her to "git orf of 'is neck."

"Thought somethink was up when I saw yer noo trousis," she said when they broke away. "Cut saucy over the trotter, ain't they!"

At my station she was in the middle of a whirl of suggestions as to shop-bells, new scales, baked chestnuts in winter, the dressing of windows, and such sordid details; but as I rose she stopped, and:

" 'Ave a poppy, Ronald?" she said, and lifted the basket to her knees.

" 'Ere, 'ave a jolly ole bunch. I don't care 'ow much I spend 's'mornin'. An', I say, Ronald, you was readin' that paper upside down. I'll send yer a bit of cake, if you like."

The Stray

It was back in the spring that I first met the fat man. I was in the garden tending a plant that a friend had given me, an Areopagitica, or some such name.

Rising from my knees I saw a hat and face sticking atop of the garden gate, like a print of old London Bridge with the traitors' sconces skewered on the spikes. The hat was a greasy bowler, and the face below it was greasy, too; a puffy face, all bristles.

The hat, I noticed, was tilted backwards off the forehead, a position forced upon it by a wen as big as a walnut, which protruded from the corner of the fat man's brow in the manner of an immature antler. Altogether, not a face to inspire trust.

"Good morning," I said, picking up a flowerpot.

"Any-rag-bottles-bone-any-ole-lumber?" said the fat man.

"Not to-day, thank you," I answered, and changed the flowerpot for a trowel. Five minutes later I looked up and the face was still there.

"What do you want?" I asked.

"Any-rag-bottles-bone-any-ole-lumber?" said the face.

"I've nothing for you," I protested, a little angry.

"Any-ole-trousis-ole-boots-medsin-bottles?" remarked the face.

"If you don't go away—" I said, and picked up another flowerpot, one with a plant in it this time.

"Mighter known," said the fat man. " 'As to wear all your ole close, don't yer?" And the face withdrew.

I was not to meet it again for a long time, not until this week, in fact, on the same day that "The Orfling" was adopted and came to live with us. This was the way of it.

135

There was a knock at the door that betokened a small child; a knock with a bounce to it, followed by a thump. Whoever it was had jumped up to the knocker, let it drop, and alighted on the doorstep. I opened the door to see a girl in a dingy red "tammy" and a pinafore with a three-cornered slit in it; a vulgar little girl who chewed a wisp of her own hair.

"Shore kitten?" she asked, and displayed a tiny morsel of black fluff that clung to her pinny with all its claws.

"No, it's not mine," I said. "I don't keep a kitten."

"It's in your garden," she persisted, and there was reproach in her voice. "Found it in your garden, 'owlin'."

"It certainly isn't mine," I answered. "You might try next door or somewhere else," and prepared to shut the door.

"Found it in your garden," repeated the girl, " 'owlin'." She rubbed her right boot up and down her left shin and waited.

"No," I said, with an air of finality, "I don't keep a kitten."

"Found it in your garden," came through the letter-box, and I went back to my book.

Ten minutes later the knocker dropped again. Another little girl with the same kitten.

"This yours?" she asked, and held it out at arm's length. I told my story once more. We did not keep a kitten. The original girl, I noticed, was waiting outside.

Five minutes later I saw them playing with the foundling, dragging a piece of string about the pavement, and saying, "Teeny Weeny Tiddles" in the tone that girls use towards babies—a squeaky treble. A woman with a basket of washing stopped to watch them. "It's lorst," said one of the girls, and the woman put her basket down.

"Come along, den!" she said. "Did she get lorsted, den?" and a lot more like that. "Diddums lose 'ems little selfums, den?"

"It's 'is, I b'lieve," said the first girl, and pointed towards the house. A boy came up. "Go an' ask 'im," suggested the woman, and I was at the door before he could knock.

" 'Ere's your moggie," said the boy, and held it out.

"Take the beastly thing away," I nearly shouted. I was getting rather tired of it. "Take it away and drown it, or keep it, or something.

Take it to the police-station." The boy put the animal down at my feet and joined the three on the pavement.

"Wotter shame," said the woman with the washing.

Then the fat man came along. He had a new hat on, and his face had lost its bristles. But I recognised the wen.

"Wossup?" he said to the small crowd.

"Kitten," said the woman. "Little black kitten. Chucked it out. Says drown it. 'Is kitten. Wotter shame!"

The fat man leaned over the fence, looked at the kitten, and then at me.

"People what 'aves cats an' can't afford to keep 'em," he said loudly, "ought to send 'em to the legal chamber." He turned to the other four, who had come closer. "They didn't oughter turn 'em out to starve. Crool shame, I call it."

"It is not my kitten, and never was my kitten," I said, speaking slowly and distinctly, and wishing heartily that I had a flowerpot.

The black imp jumped on to the step between my feet, and rubbed its sides against my slippers, making a bubbly noise like boiling water.

"Look at it," said the fat man. "Knows 'im. Knows its way about. 'Fectionate lil blighter. Crool shame, I call it. People what 'aves cats an' can't afford a few fish-bones didn't oughter turn 'em out in the street to starve." A telegraph boy came across to look into the matter. "Says it ain't 'is," explained the fat man to the newcomer. "Look at it makin' a fuss of 'im. 'Fectionate lil blighter."

The kitten was bubbling away on the doorstep, and saying "Proo-Prow" every second, while the fat man exhorted his audience.

"That kitten knows, it does. 'E knows. If anybody says as that ain't their kitten, e's a liar. Bin chucked out, that's what's the matter. Chucked out to starve. Crool shame, I call it. People what 'aves cats what they can't afford to keep oughter take 'em to the legal chamber, they did."

The kitten bubbled harder than ever. "Keep it up," it said. "Keep it up, and I'm adopted."

"Pore little dee-yer," said the woman. "Wotter shame." Truly, when I came to look at it, I thought some milk would not be amiss. Its nose was sharp as a pen.

"You'd think 'as people what lived in a respectable neighbourhood could keep a lil kitten, you would," said the fat man. "A bit o' fish and some scraps. P'raps 'e don't 'ave no scraps. It's crool, that's what it is. Crool!"

"Go it," purred the kitten, "lay it on thick. He's melting."

"A pore man 'd git prosecuted," went on the fat man. "One lore for the rich. Anybody else'd say the same. People what 'aves cats what they can't afford to keep oughter be made to, they did, so there!"

"Swat I bin sayin' all along," said the woman. The mite certainly looked very pathetic. I tickled it between the ears and it sang aloud.

"Knows 'im!" said the fat man in triumph. "Knows 'im right enough. See! Said so soon's I sore it." He wiped his mouth on a red handkerchief after that. "People what 'aves cats—" I took the kitten in and adopted it. A muffled voice trickled through the letter-box.

" 'At's 'is, all right. Tried to do the dirty on it. Soon showed 'im! People what 'aves cats what they can't afford to keep—" I went into the garden and fetched a flowerpot.

The Skivvy

Adversity is almost the only circumstance which will make two strangers in a train speak to each other. The empty matchbox, the flat tobacco pouch, these will open the mouths of men who otherwise would travel from London to Orkney, each reading the advertisements over the other's head.

There are, of course, other methods of starting a conversation, but they are risky. You may tread on someone's feet and find him quite a nice chap. Trifles like this have led to lasting friendships.

It was through some such accident that I met the girl with the red arms at half-past nine on a recent Sunday evening. She sat next to me in the train, reading in a large book which she held close under her nose. Of her general appearance I remember nothing, except that her rather pretty hair was drawn tight off her forehead, and screwed up behind after the manner of a charity school child. There were none of those stray wisps playing about her ears that make a plain face so pretty.

The sleeves of her dress finished at the elbow, and her arms were all red and coarse. In her lap lay a screwed-up handkerchief, a pair of white gloves rolled into a ball, a purse, and a screwed-up bag of toffee.

Atop of these articles she presently laid the book; and, after dabbing at her eyes with the handkerchief, went to sleep. It was a troubled doze, and I watched the book slide and slide until it thumped to the floor. I picked it up (it was "The Shadow of Ashlydyat"), and the girl said she was sorry, and went to sleep again. Within the next five minutes I recovered severally the toffee, the gloves, and the book.

"Dunno why I keep droppin' off," she said. "See me goin' past my station in a minute, and that'll do it." I offered to nudge her when

139

we arrived at her destination, but she thought she could keep awake if she tried.

The window of the carriage was splashed with slanting rows of rain drops that blurred the night lights of Camden Town.

" 'Tain't 'alf comin' down, is it?" said the girl, and cleaned a semicircular patch of the window with her handkerchief. "Like billy-o!" With her nose against the glass, she peered into the outer darkness.

"My day out," she added. "Dunno 'ow it is, but it's rained on my last seven days out. An' we only get one a munf. 'Tain't 'alf all right, is it? 'S'mornin' when I was clearin' away the brekfus' it was fine enough, but soon's I goes upstairs to dress down it comes like billy-o.

"The ole man—you know, the boss, the guv'nor—'e was as pleased as anythink. Stood a-lookin' out of the winder and whistlin', an' walkin' up an' down the room, an' stickin' 'is stummick out as if 'e'd made it rain. 'What we been wantin',' 'e says. 'Do the lawn no end o' good.'

"We only gets one day a munf, you know, 'leven to ten, an' one evenin' a week, seven to ten; so I 'opes 'is jolly ole lawn gets struck by lightning." For a while she was silent, as if debating whether she had not perhaps gone a little too far. Or, maybe, it had come over her that there was some impropriety in her talking thus to a stranger. Evidently not, for "Joo eat sweets?" she asked, and rummaged among Mrs. Henry Wood and the purse and the handkerchief.

I decided that I did, and she held the bag while I struggled to detach a piece of toffee. But toffee and bag were glued fast together, and my portion was only broken off by a vigorous application of the mass to the heel of her boot.

For some moments we chewed in silence. It was only by studying the undulatory movements of the girl's face that I was able to eat my portion at all without lockjaw setting in. The stuff had a tendency to cling; and the great thing, I found, was to keep it on the move.

The girl chewed on for some time, looking me up and down rather curiously, and then spoke. This she accomplished by working the toffee into her cheek, where it made a bump like a gumboil.

"You a clurk?" she asked suddenly. I told her I was not.

"Look like one," she said; "that 'igh collar an' all. Just like a clurk. Thought you was. No offence, you know! Don't mind, do yer?" I said I did not mind, and we had some more toffee.

"I 'ad a young man once," the girl went on. " 'E was a clurk. Nice 'igh collar and all that. Always neat an' tidy. You know! Smoked a wooden pipe, same's you, an' wore a 'ard 'at every day. But 'e give me the chuck, 'e did." She shifted the toffee from one cheek to the other.

"My fault. I swanked 'im, and 'e found me out. Too good for me, 'e was. Respectable, y'know. Class!

" 'Is father was a manager or somethink. I don't blame 'im, though. When a young man finds out that a girl's bin a-kiddin' of 'im on, you can't expect 'e's goin' to keep on with 'er after that, can yer?

"Y'see, I met 'im outside the Bon Marsh one Sunday night last summer. Didn't know 'im, y'know. Just met 'im like—like—well, like you do meet people, see?

"I was goin' by, an' 'e said, 'Goo' night, miss,' an' took off 'is 'at, an' I looked round an' see 'im lookin' round; an' I walked slower an' looked round again, an' 'e caught me up.

"Course, I was dressed diff'rent to what I am now. These are my old things for when it's rainin'. I 'ad on all white, then; skirt, an' stockin's, an' shoes. Dinkey! You know!

"But 'e found out. Mighter known 'e would, but I didn't think.

"We went out together for nearly free munce. 'Ad nice times, too, goin' to the Park, an' Kew Gardens, an' all that.

" 'E always 'ad plenty o' money. You know, 'nough to 'ave a good time, an' ices, an' go in the side shows, an' all that, an' 'e was a bit of a toff in 'is way, an' I didn't want to lose 'im. So I told 'im I was a nurse, 'cos I knew 'e wouldn't go out with a skivvy. An' 'e found out.

"Called round one night to see me. I told 'im not to, but 'e called round an' went to the front door, an' 'e asked for me. An' the parlourmaid told 'im to go to the tradesmen's entrance an' ask for the kitchenmaid, an' that did it ... I didn't see 'im no more.

"Still, it was my fault. 'Is people 'ad a 'ouse all to theirselves, an' it stands to reason 'e wouldn't go out with a skivvy, don't it?

"But I 'ad a good time while it lasted. Shows you what comes of tellin' lies an' swankin'."

After a pause, "I don't care," she went on defiantly, "I 'ad a lot of fine outin's with 'im … When you only go out once a munf, you don't stand much chance of gittin' off, do yer? Specially when it's like this 'ere. An' I'm 22 in October."

The Accident

For many of the minor tragedies of life the sufferer seldom gets his full meed of sympathy. Custom has decreed that certain little things that happen to all of us shall be considered funny. Pimples are funny, seasickness is funny, toothache is funny, mumps are funny. There are scores of them; mirth-provoking complaints that tickle the ribs of the bystander until he roars; but the point of which the sufferer cannot see.

If you have been seasick, you will know just how merry a business it is; and although you may keep serious in its presence, you will assuredly laugh at the thought of it later on. It is a standard jest; every time the Channel Tunnel recurs, and whenever else possible. That particular joke (illustrated) of the hot mutton always fetches them. A description of the sufferer, too, his pale green face, his fear that he is going to die; his fear, at a later stage, that he is not; this will always cause endless amusement.

I have tried hard to see the joke about mumps, but in vain. Yet, in the hands of Mr. George Robey or Mr. Heath Robinson, mumps would be side-splitting.

Pimples, too. There was, long ago, a popular song whose refrain ran:

We knew her by the pimple,
The pimple on her nose.

Can you imagine anything more tragic than a young lady, priding herself on her complexion maybe, who, on the eve of a party for which she has a new frock, develops a pimple on her nose? (Now laugh!) I see her before her glass, dab-dabbing with her powder-puff, trying to tone it down; giving up in despair, and weeping her eyes all red. There go her dreams, her conquests, her chances of marriage, everything; laid low by a pimple.

She knows everyone would laugh. They would be sorry for her, but they would laugh. Because pimples are funny, forsooth. You get one just where the top of your collar comes, and see if it is funny. Or find another man who has one in that same situation, and see if it isn't funny.

In the same class I would put black eyes. Absolute screams, black eyes are. Some music-hall artists dare not go on the stage without one at least.

One of the finest I ever saw was being worn by a tram conductor. It was an early tram, and from the corner seat by the door I had a good look at it. At the centre of the trouble, just above and below the eye, it was black. Not jet black quite; but a blue-black, like a ripe grape. Towards the cheek bone this paled to a neutral tint (Payne's Grey, I think it is called); and this again ran out to a washy green at the edge, with a faint pink aureole. It was really awfully funny.

It took up all his left eye and trespassed a little across the bridge of his nose; and its shape was like a map of the Isle of Wight.

The conductor leaned back against the stairway and whistled "The Children's Home." Perhaps he had forgotten his disfigurement, though it looked very painful.

Still whistling, he crooked his knees and began to fill up his waybill, sucking the point of his pencil stump between the tremolos. The tram stopped; and "Gobble-Gobble Road," he sang out.

A timekeeper sauntered towards the tram.

"Mornin', 'Arry!" he said, then caught sight of the eye. " 'Allo, where'd you get that?" he asked with a laugh. "Stopped one?"

"Cricket ball," said the conductor. "One of my youngsters. Caught me a proper smack, too." The timekeeper expressed his thoughts in a long, liquid whistle, and the tram moved on.

The conductor said nothing, but wrote hard on his waybill, and his lips moved. Presently we stopped again. "Gobble-Gobble Square," he called. Another conductor mounted the step, swinging a blue enamel can. He was going upstairs when he saw the eye. "Coo!" he said. "That's a beauty, ain't it?"

"You can 'ave it, if you like," said the conductor, but the other only laughed.

"Where'd you get it?" he asked.

"Cupboard door," said the first. "Somebody left it open. Walked slap into it in the dark. Wot yer laughin' at?" But the other man had run upstairs, convulsed; and when the tram stopped for somebody who did not want it, the conductor nearly wrenched the bell-cord out of its fastenings. "Gobble-Gobble Corner," he called; caught me looking at the eye, and glared. I studied the fare-board closely.

The next kind inquiry came from a taxi-driver who drew alongside, but it brought no solution to the mystery of the accident.

"What a mouse!" cried the cabman. "Why don't you get a seppyration order, mate?" And, coward like, he threw a lever over, and bumped away to a sound of stripping cogwheels. I was afraid to look at the conductor.

At the next stop (it was Gobble-Gobble Square, I think) we were boarded by an inspector, to whom, of course, one must be respectful.

"Hallo, had an accident?" he asked, with a kindly grin. "How'd you manage that?"

"Birdcage," said the conductor, and there was just a touch of venom in his voice. " 'Anging up the birdcage. Missed the 'ook. Wallop! Right on the bridge of my nose."

"I see," said the inspector. "Tickets, please." He signed the book, and swung to the footboard. "You should be careful of those birdcages," he said. "Nasty things. Try a bit of raw beef." The conductor was very wrath, and turned to me for sympathy.

"There ain't no pleasin' 'em. Can't 'ave a black eye now, but what everybody don't want to know the ins and outs of it," he said. "An' then they laugh! See anything to laugh at?"

"Certainly not," I answered, suppressing a giggle. "I've had one myself, so I know."

" 'Ow did you come by it?" he asked.

"Er—fell over a dustpan," I said. "At least, I think it was a dustpan, but I forget."

145

"I 'adn't thought of that," said the conductor.

At the next stop I prepared to leave the tram. "Then there's the broom handle," I said. "You can get a nasty whack on the face by stepping on the head of a broom. Those swing doors, too, are beastly contrivances." I stepped on to the footboard.

"By the way, conductor," I said, "how *did* you get that black eye—really?" He slipped his fingers to his coat buttons.

"You wait a jiffy," said the conductor, "an' I'll show you!"

The Last Straw

With the reddening of the creeper leaves, the "fiery funeral of foliage old," and the coming of the morning fogs, the timid man may well begin to feel a little nervous. He has arrived at a crisis in his year.

Sooner or later, within a day or two perhaps, he must discard his straw hat, and take once more to the sombre bowler against the rigours of winter.

No small thing, this. The day of the exchange must be well judged. For if he leave it too long, he will find himself one cold morning the only man in all London still wearing his straw. People in the train will look at him, their smirks tinged with pity, and youth will make rude remarks.

Something similar happens in the springtime, when a few bright days will fill the windows with summer attire. But then again the human butterfly is nervous of venturing forth too soon from his chrysalid case. Suppose he should leave home one morning in his nice new straw, and find himself a pioneer, with young barbarians asking loudly for information as to who robbed the donkey of his breakfast. Useless for him to point out that donkeys do not eat straw.

How the hot blushes would race over his body! How he would find every eye upon him; hear giggles where no giggles were; yes, and even be driven into buying a new bowler, and having the premature straw sent home.

Recognising these possibilities, he waits for someone else to break the ice, and when three men in ten have taken the plunge, he will be ready to make a fourth. That day it will rain.

I have been looking sadly at my hat for the past few days; and I am afraid the end is near. I recall its pristine creaminess and beauty when I bought it, its fine varnish, correct crown and brim, and perfect band. But look at it now! It has been caught out without an umbrella more than once; and its roof has a dip towards the centre. Nor is its brim horizontal, except in parts. The straw is sunburnt and grimy, and the varnish has long ago gone.

Inside the brim I find, tucked behind the leather band, a sheet of newspaper neatly folded (mine was ever an awkward head; neither 6 7-8 nor 7), and the date on it is May 17. So I have had my money's worth. And now it is good-bye.

Some there are who resort to binoxalate of potash or half a lemon, and rejuvenate their hats for the opening of next spring; but if in the dark days of December I happened upon this relic, I might weep for the summer of yesteryear. And I like to celebrate spring with a new thatch. There is something cheap and nasty about the idea of welcoming the hawthorn in a chemically bleached straw.

Therefore I decided last week that Mr. Pettigrew should have it. I think his name is Pettigrew, or it may be Merrydew; I cannot be sure. You see, he has very few teeth in front, and it never sounds twice alike. Sometimes I think it is Featherfew, but that is when he is smoking. Anyway, he was very glad of the hat.

He was sitting on an upturned flowerpot when I carried it to him. The grass, he said, was too wet to cut, so I suppose he was waiting for it to dry.

"This is a melancholy occasion, Mr. Merrydew," I began; "a very melancholy occasion." I cleared my throat.

"Dear, dear!" said the gardener. "And when's to be the funeral?" He is a little deaf, I think. I went on.

"Unaccustomed as I am to public speaking—" Mr Merrydew stood up, took off his hat, and twiddled it in his hands.

"With the uprooting of the last petunia," I said; "when the big, fat spiders hang their dew-pearled snares between the Michaelmas daisies; when the dahlia blooms no longer offer refuge to the vile earwig; then, oh, Mr. Featherfew, man, like to some of the lesser animals, bethinks him of his warmer underclothes.

The summer's throbbing chant is done,
And mute the choral antiphon.

Presently will come the churlish chiding of the winter's wind, and it wants scarce three months to Christmas."

"Law, sir!" said Mr. Honeydew. "And me not got 'arf the bulbses in yet, an' the border not digged over."

I was determined to have the thing done properly, so I ignored the materialistic interruption.

"Therefore, Mr. Pettigrew," I continued, "in common with many of my fellows, I am preparing to dispense with this battered relic of a bygone heat-wave." I produced the hat from behind me.

"Far be it from me to underestimate the value of your long and faithful services—"

"Are you supposed to be giving me the sack?" asked Mr. Featherfew.

"—and this hat, the emblem of a defunct solstice, is, I know, but a meagre recompense for your—er—your long and faithful services. Winter, Mr. Pettigrew, is a-coming in, and—"

"I must push along with them there iersince and chewlips," mused Mr. Pettigrew. " 'Fore we know where we are, we'll 'ave the frostses down on us, an' then we shall be done in the eye in a manner of speakin'."

In the face of such interruptions, eloquence must fail. It was like the ever-present "voice" at a political meeting.

"If you won't let me give you this old hat in a fit and becoming manner," I said, "take the jolly old thing and get on with your work."

"Oh, the 'at!" said Mr. Merrydew. "Is that for me? Why, I ain't 'arf wore out the one you give me larsh year yet. A good enough 'at it is still; with munce an' munce of 'ard wear in it." To prove his words he held it out to me.

To think that I had ever worn that grimy, misshapen three-and-ninepence-worth. Its brim hung down like a penthouse, its roof was semi-detached; and if Mr. Merrydew had had any hair atop of his head, it must have poked through towards the light.

"Throw it away," I said. "Put it in the dustbin, or the cold frame, or the hotbed. Abolish it, and take this. You shall never want for hats while I have an old one to spare." Mr. Pettigrew was overwhelmed.

"Thankin' you one an' all," he said with an ungainly bob. "It's lucky you take the same size as me." He tried it on, and threw the old wreck away, looking after it regretfully.

"What you was sayin' about the passin' of the seasons is very true, sir," he said presently. "We goes from snowdrops to crocuses, from crocuses to daffs an' iersince, an' so on, to the Canterbury bells an' sweet williams. Then comes the roses an' things, an' then the Michaelmas daisies, an' so on. Chrysants is last, and then we gets the bulbses in. An' so we goes on from year to year. Always busy, always a-plantin' or a-diggin' up. Wunnerful, the works of Nature, ain't they?" He studied the lining of his new old hat.

"Wunnerful thing when you think of it. When I'm dead an' gone, you'll maybe give your old 'ats to the next man you 'as in. You'll maybe give away p'raps as many as fifty old strore 'ats, an' then *you'll* be dead an' gone. Wunnerful, ain't it?"

The Prodigy

Apart from the fragment of pink nougat which adhered to his left cheek, Ronald was not a remarkable child. He was dressed in complete black velvet, with heavy leather boots, and a broad-brimmed straw hat labelled "H.M.S. Formidable." A closer examination of his face revealed the fact that in addition to the sweetmeat his cheeks provided anchorage for a few crumbs and a jam smear.

He came in with a rush and a large grandmother, flustered and out of breath. She flopped into a seat and did breathing exercises for perhaps a minute. Then, when she could, she said to the boy:

"Nearly missed it, didn't we, Ronnie? Only just caught it, didn't we?"

"Puffer," said the boy.

Granny, whose beads rattled as she recovered her breath, now began to look about her. "I s'pose it's all right," she said aloud. "This a Elephant, young man?" It was, and she settled herself again.

"Puffer," said the boy.

"Yes, dear," said the woman. "Nice puffer. Goes shoo-shoo." She looked out of the window, then jumped up hurriedly and grabbed the child.

"What a mercy!" she exclaimed to everybody. "What a mercy! 'Ere'm I a-sittin' with my back to the injin'." She staggered across the carriage, and settled herself once more. "Don't wonder I was feelin' sort of all-overish," she said at large. "There you are, dear. Now see the nice puffer. See'm go shoo-shoo."

"Puffer," said the boy, and knelt on the seat, his nose and lips flattened against the window-pane.

Breathing on the glass and inscribing hieroglyphics on the dulled surface soon palled on Ronald, and he turned round hurriedly and sat down, wiping his boots on the lady next to him.

"Naughty!" said granny. "Made the nice lady all dirty," and dabbed at the miry patch with her handkerchief. "I'm sure I'm very sorry, mum," she said. But it did not matter in the least, was of no consequence at all; and before they had been apologising to one another for more than a minute they had known each other for years.

"Your little boy?" inquired the nice lady.

"My son's, mum," said granny, swelling a little. "My son's, an' as bright a child—really, you'd never believe. The things he says, an' only two an' a 'alf. That forward! Speak to the nice lady, Ronnie. Say your potries."

"Puffer," said Ronnie, and clapped his feet together rapidly.

" 'E knows," said his grandmother. "Say 'e don't know! Talk when 'e's in the 'umour right enough. Licker to me where 'e gets it all from. What 'ave I got in this bag, Ronnie?"

"Boo-boos," said Ronnie.

"There! What'd I tell you? Sweets, 'e means. Calls 'em all bull's-eyes. Knowin' ain't the word."

"Boo-boos," said Ronnie, and granny dived into her Dorothy bag.

During the next five minutes the sweetmeat was alternately sucked and inspected, considerable addition being made to the alluvial deposit on the child's cheeks.

"Now let granny wipe your mouth … There's a little man! An' now say your potries to the nice lady. 'E knows all the nurs'ry rhymes off by 'eart, an' songs an' 'yms. Sings by the hour, 'e does; don't you, Ronnie?"

"Puffer," said Ronnie. "Shoo-shoo!"

"They know!" said granny with emphasis. "Don't tell me they don't know. Now be a good boy, there's a dear, an' say your nice potries to the nice lady."

"Boo-boos," remarked the boy.

"No more till you've said your pieces," said granny, and swept him on to her lap. "Now then, come along! Mary—" she waited for the child to fill in the blank; but that failing, she filled it in herself to encourage the boy. "Mary—'adder—liddle—"

"Puffer," said Ronnie.

" 'E knows, you know. Only the fit ain't on 'im. When the fit's on 'im you can't stop 'im," said granny by way of apology.

"Now come along, deeyer; say your potries for the nice lady. Mary—'adder—liddle—"

"Glob," said the child.

"There!" chimed in granny, all smiles. "There! What'd I tell you? The knowingest youngster as ever was. Go on, deeyer. Its fleecers— whiters—"

"Glob," from Ronnie.

"The pet!" said granny, and half-smothered him. "Now another one. Liddle Jack—"

There was a guttural sound from Ronald that might have been understood by grandmotherly pride to resemble "Horner," but to the unbiassed listener it sounded rather like hiccoughs.

"Satiner—corner, eatin'—"

"Grmph," said Ronnie.

"—whey," finished granny. "There's a love! Doesn't he say it nicely? The artfullest young 'un, 'e was. Go on, deeyer. Long cummer—spider—" (she really thought the boy was saying it all) "— an' sat down—"

"Boo-boos," demanded Ronald.

"When you've said it, deeyer. An' sat down—"

"Boo-boos," reiterated the child.

"All right, then, 'cos you've bin a good boy, an' said your potries for the nice lady. 'Alf a minute." The Dorothy bag was requisitioned once more.

"D'you think all that peppermint is good for him?" asked the lady for whose benefit the entertainment was arranged.

"Law, bless your 'eart," said granny. "I don't make no odds about that. 'Is mother don't let him 'ave 'em; but I says, 'When 'e's out with me 'e's goin' to enjoy 'isself.' 'E's goin' to 'ave a good time when 'e's with 'is ole gran, ain't you, Ronnie? That's right! If 'e don't 'ave it now, 'e won't never get it. 'Appiest time of his life, if 'e did but know it." She sighed hugely.

"Mother says I spoil 'im; but I tell 'er I knows best about that. Seven I've brought up, an' all thrivin', an' out an' doin' well. An' a bull's-eye never 'urt 'um, did it, Ronnie? Let granny wipe 'is mouth all nice an' clean. There! Now say your other piece."

"Boo-boos," said Ronald, and reached out at the piece of nougat with his tongue.

"Not till you've said it," remarked granny, getting the bag ready. "Come along, now. Ick'ry, dick'ry—"

"Dock," said the child, as plainly as you or I could; while grandmother nearly fell off her seat. He had really said it, clearly and completely.

" 'Ark at that," said granny. "Just 'ark. Ick'ry, dick'ry—"

"Dock," added Ronald.

"Jever 'ear the like?" asked the woman. "Didn't I tell you? An' only two an' a 'alf. Say it again, deeyer. Ick'ry, dick'ry—"

"Boo-boos," said the boy; but his admirer wanted more.

"The mouse—ran up—the—"

"Boo-boos," protested Ronald.

" 'E's tired, bless 'im," said granny. "S'pose I didn't ought to worry 'im to say no more. There y'are, deeyer; there's your sweeties. Two for sayin' your potries to the nice lady. Now, don't put 'em both in at once. An' what d'you say? No! Wait a minute. What d'you say, first?"

"Boo-boos," was all Ronald said, and put both in at once.

Bookworms

Promise of a wet week-end will usually find me sitting on the pulp box in Mr. Merman's shop, and turning over the derelict volumes there in the uncertain hope of a "find." To the pulp box come at length those poor, heart-broken books that will never sell, even in a second-hand bookshop on a wet Saturday night. At intervals they are sent to a paper mill to be smashed into pulp and made into new and, we will hope, more fortunate volumes.

I like to turn over the contents of the pulp box, and, in spite of Mr. Merman's keen eye, have sometimes found among the dead brains a live little book worth the finding. In such cases Mr. Merman is a real sportsman, and what one finds among the pulp one buys at pulp prices. But he does not leave much, and a Kate Greenaway almanac at twopence is the best bargain I have made for some months.

From his perch halfway up the stepladder Mr. Merman discourses of books and bookselling.

"The position of mentor to the buyers and hirers of second-hand novels is no sinecure," he says. "There are responsibilities. This afternoon, for instance, a woman came to me for the fourth part of 'The Hearthrug Hour,' a weekly publication that died in 1889. It appeared she had bought the first three numbers from me some months ago, and had become interested in the serial story; and now she is tramping from one bookshop to another trying to find out what happened to the heroine in the fourth instalment.

"For all I know I have wrecked her home. I see her two babies (they were outside the shop in a perambulator) going neglected and hungry; I see her husband sockless, his dinner uncooked; while she wears out pair after pair of boots in a vain search for the end of the story."

He descended the ladder to take twopence from a tram conductor for Lang's "Origins of Religion," and was making himself comfortable on a pile of "Self-Educators" when a woman came into the shop.

She was of the type known as well-preserved, inclining to buxomness; and her figure was hung all about with expensive jewellery, so that she jingled as she walked.

"I am willing to wager," said Mr. Merman, "that she wants either a treatise on totemism or 'The Guitar Made Easy in Twenty Lessons'." But he was wrong. Her voice met him halfway.

"I—ah—want a—ah—book," she said.

"Yes, madam; and the subject?" asked Mr. Merman.

"Oh—er—just something to read, you know. What have you got?" She jingled her way towards the fiction shelves (the "Sobs and Sighs" Mr. Merman calls them), took down a volume, and opened it in two or three places.

"Looks int'restin'," she mused, read half a page, and shut it with a bang. "No," she said, "not that sort. You see, it's for my daughter, and one must be careful, you know. Have you a—ah—love story? Something not too parful. Oh, yes! I've heard of this one. Very good, isn't it? I think that'll do. You see, my niece— Oh, and I may as well take the other one, too. Tuppence a volume a week, isn't it? Thank you!" She rattled away with the parful book and the other.

"There is an expression of incredulity much in use among the lower classes," said Mr. Merman, "which would seem to meet the case. In similar circumstances I have heard them say 'Wow-wow!' with the accent on the last 'Wow.' I wonder whether it was really for her niece or her daughter."

His speculations were cut into by the entry of a tiny servant girl in stiff white apron, lace cap, and streamers that were horizontal with speed.

"Please, missus wants a book and a shilling's worth of coppers for the gas."

"Any idea what kind of book?" asked Mr. Merman.

"Don't care much, only let it be a long 'un," said the girl. "Then she'll stop in bed a-Sunday mornin'. One of the fattest you got. Oh, and please she says she wants a love story like the last."

Mr. Merman took down a volume and ran through the pages. "Here is a beautiful love story," he said; "five hundred and sixty pages, close print."

"Does it end 'appy?" asked the girl. "Does it all come out in the wash in the last act? Them sad ones makes 'er as cross as a bear with a sore 'ead. ' 'Appy-ever-afters' is what she likes. Then I can get on with my work."

The bookseller turned to the last page. "Yes," he said. "This seems all right. The lady—the heroine, you know—falls—let me see—no, throws herself on to the gentleman's shoulder in a paroxysm of glad tears. How will that do?"

"Sounds a bit damp, don't it?" said the girl. "I like—she likes plenty of dangers an' perils, an' all that. ' "Aha!" he cried, an' stabbed 'er to the 'eart.' You know! ... 'Ow about this one? 'For Sword an' Sweet'eart; a Story of Love Triumphant.' That's the 'ammer!" She ran her eye down the chapter headings. "Looks like gore through, don't it? An' I don't know if she wants gore. Poisonin' I know she don't mind, an' that other stuff—int-something—intrigue, ain't it? You know, schemin' an' swankin', an' kidnappin', an' then gettin' married at the village church in the last chapter, all covered with roses. Got one of those?"

Mr. Merman put his head in the pulp box for a while. He emerged a few seconds later, quite recovered, and regretted that he did not think he had such a book.

"Jew always do your thinkin' in that there packin' case?" asked the girl. Then impatiently: "Come on, Willie. I got to be in by ten." She moved along the shelves, mumbling the titles to herself.

" 'The Bride in the Black Veil.' I 'ad that last week. 'Sin an' Simplicity,' 'Shadowed Love,' 'Burnt Ashes.' I say, what a lot of ole duds you've got 'ere. Want a spring clean ... 'Allo, 'ere's one! 'A Daughter of Darkness.' That sounds all right. Chap. I., 'The Body in the Moat'; Chap. II., 'The Jewelled Berlade.' " She turned to the end of the book. "Chap. LX., 'The Mortuary-Keeper's Love Story'; Chap.

LXI., 'Orange Blossom.' Now you're talkin', old son. This'll do. An' now those coppers for the gas. Better let's 'ave two bob's worth. She'll want 'em."

The Stranger

London within the three-mile radius is a dangerous country for the man who wears gaiters. Be he the most sophisticated of Cockneys, let him stand for five minutes and stare with wide eyes at the fountains of Trafalgar Square, and straightaway one of his father's oldest friends will happen along, and offer to hold his purse for old times' sake.

If, in addition to wearing gaiters, he chews a straw in a meditative and cud-like manner, he will find the streets thronged with men who met him at last year's Bath and West, jostling for places with life-long friends of his brother and cousin.

It is a great game. You just stand straddle-legged, and gaze and gaze at the Nelson Column, running your eyes slowly upwards from the lions at the bottom to the pigeons at the top, opening your mouth wider and wider as your head goes backwards. This attitude is supposed to be typical of the countryman in town. What you do with the straw when you open your mouth I have not discovered.

When your man has found you, the first thing to do is to put your hand on your watch as if you had a pain. Then you ask him if that be the Albert Memorial or Cleopatra's Needle. But don't blame me if he makes answer, requesting you not to "come it." Most probably the fault is with you; the overdoing of the innocent, sheep-like expression, or a lack of the true pastoral air in the chewing of your straw.

There was a fine morning one day this week, a few hours left over from summer; and having spent the best part of a month slopping through the mud of London, I decided to make holiday, and slop for a day through the mud of the country.

To that end I got myself up in a pair of cloth gaiters and a soft hat, very shapeless and very comfortable. These little touches are necessary to convince you that you really have got a day off. No one could possibly go nutting or ratting or maying in a hard bowler hat.

As the bus swept westwards down Ludgate-hill I turned in my seat to get sight of St. Paul's, on whose new-gilded cross the sun made a brave show.

"St. Paul's, that is," said a man in the seat behind me. I expressed my thanks, and continued to gaze.

"Fine old place," he added. "Sir Christopher Wren, you know. Built it after the Great Fire." And then it was I went astray.

"Was that so?" I remarked, and recalled, with possibly too great a show of innocence, that I had read about it somewhere in a book.

"Interesting ride, this," said the man presently. "When you do it a dozen times a day you forget its interest. But to a stranger, of course— I'll come and sit beside you, if I may." His was not a top hat to inspire confidence; it looked as though it had been dressed with brilliantine, and the brim was very flat; but I moved up a little to make room.

"I'll point out the sights to you as we go along if you like," he said. "Stopping in London long?" Well, I could not say exactly how long. His cross-examination became more searching. Yes, I had some friends in London, and was going as far as Victoria on this bus. That was curious. He was going to Victoria, to see—er—to see his solicitors, and after that he was free for the day. Had I come far? Oh, a Sussex man. Yes, I knew Hastings, and had spent some time at Rye. Well, now, that was strange, that was. Why, he was born at Rye, in What-d'you-call-it Street. Pulled down now, he thought. Whatever was it? Forget his own name next. Down by the—er—down by the bank. Dear, dear! He had it on the tip of his tongue a minute ago.

I made a suggestion. No, that wasn't it. I made another. Of course! Watchtower-street, it was. (There is no such street in Rye, by the way.) Big house with the creeper on it. Perhaps I knew it. Anyway, he was glad to meet a Sussex man. Gave me a sort of claim on him, and all that.

For a little while he said nothing, but sat watching me as I endeavoured to show a keen interest in what was passing in the street below. Then suddenly he turned round and drew my attention to Temple Bar, just retreating out of sight.

"That's the Crimean Memorial," he said. "Queen Victoria on one side; Tsar of Russia on the other. On top is the Griffin, the straight Griffin." He looked searchingly at me, but I stared all I knew at this new wonder.

I could hardly make him out. The game, as I understood it, was not played this way. He must know that even in Sussex there are picture postcards. Doubtless it would develop before we reached Victoria, and then I would show him what a fool he had been.

In the Strand I learned where Dick Whittington lived and died (his cat, stuffed, you may be surprised to learn, is in the British Museum). I also saw the very wine shop where Oliver Cromwell ducked the Duke of Clarence in a butt of malmsey; and the spot where Guy Fawkes first sold fireworks.

"Trafalgar Square," he said presently. This, thought I, is too well known to be lied about, but, "Those fountains are filled with water brought straight from Trafalgar's Bay. Where the big battle was fought, you know." ("You'll overdo it in a minute," I said to myself.)

In Whitehall he was magnificent, and once I nearly laughed; but as an exhibition of leg-pulling it was too lavish, and would not have deceived a fisherman from the Outer Hebrides. In Victoria-street I decided that the matter must be cleared up.

"Well, chummy," he said, when I put the question to him, "it's like this. The way you looked at St. Paul's I thought I was on to a good thing. But you let me draw you out too much.

"If I'd wanted to sell you a pup or plant a stumer on you I shouldn't have told you things. I should have taken it for granted that you knew your way about. And I should have let you know that I knew. See? Then you made two bloomers. You let me see the label inside your hat. Chiswick, wasn't it? And you gave the conductor tuppence without saying where you wanted to go, and then didn't look at your ticket. That made me suspicious. So I tried you with the Griffin. You ought to have corrected me. Everybody knows Temple Bar.

"But the way you lapped it up! When you swallowed that about Dick Whittington, I knew you were too good to be true. So I laid it on thick, just for fun, to try and make you give yourself away. I must say you stuck it very well; too well, in fact. You ought not to have believed that yarn about the fountains. Wasn't bad for an impromptu, was it? Oh, and there was another thing. You didn't look round when that horse fell down. So altogether, as a village idiot you're a rotten failure. I knew you for one of the boys before you'd said a dozen words. 'He's fly,' I said to myself.

"Still, it's been a pleasant journey. You getting down now? Well, look here. We understand one another, don't we? Now I've got an absolutely red-hot thing for the Cambridgeshire. This is the straightology, this is. It's the good goods, and—let's step across the road and talk it over."

But I thought not.

The Reformer

With the train (and that the last but one) running across the bridge as I ran under it, I knew my chances of catching it were small; but although the guard's whistle shrilled as I bought my ticket, yet I did not entirely give up hope. Sometimes, when a train is delayed in the station, the guard will blow his whistle at intervals of half a minute, to fan the dying hopes of the passengers.

Knowing this, I pelted up the stairs several at a time, and at the top went up one stair that did not exist; only to see the red rear lights fading at the other end of the platform, with, as it were, their thumbs to their noses. So I sat on a seat and put my thumb to my nose to show how little I cared.

When I had recovered my breath, I noticed another object on the seat beside me—a dark, crumpled, and shapeless mass of shadows, from which at intervals issued little grunts. Ours is an economical line, and between the trains they turn the lights down; so that until this thing spoke I did not recognise it for a human being.

First the legs sprawled outwards, then the head rose from the chest, and the whole resolved itself into a man in evening dress, who turned and looked long at me.

"Was that last train the last train?" he asked. I told him that the next would be the last.

"I heard that one come in," he said, "but I was too comfortable to get up. So I let it go. What does it matter? A hundred years hence, when you and I behind the veil are cast, and all that sort of thing, it will matter still less. I was comfortable, and that doesn't happen to a man many times in one's life. Therefore, why heed the rumble of the distant train?" He struck himself heavily on the chest, and relapsed into silence; then sidled along the bench towards me, and plucked me by the sleeve. His voice was low and serious now.

"That star above the signal box is Jupiter," he said. "It's got four moons and is ever so many million miles away. I forget how many, but I've got it in a book at home. And yet you worry! What does it matter? What does anything matter? If you lose your job or get summoned for your rates, or catch a cold on the chest, you worry pounds of flesh off yourself. Yet there goes old Jupiter, still getting on with it, buzzing about. What's it matter? Same with politics.

"Have you noticed that all the porters on this line are Socialists? Well, it is so. I've been looking. They all wear red ties." He increased his hold on my coat and reduced his voice to an earnest whisper.

"Now, in my opinion, Socialism, while admirable in theory, is impracticable. Until we can wipe out the human equation, ob-ob-obliterate the individual, and make—but what's the good of talking?"

I said I didn't know.

From the pocket of his overcoat he drew a handful of walnuts, and crushed one between his teeth.

"One of these days," he said, "Nature will evolve the perfect walnut—without shell, without skin, and with a pinch of salt on it. At present they are not a nut that one can eat with comfort in the dark. But talking of Socialism—"

"Let us keep to walnuts," I interposed.

"Very well," he said, "we will talk of walnuts. Now, I have tried every sort of politics, only to come empty away. They seem to think that such things as Home Rule, and education, and back-to-back houses, and swine fever, are the be-all and end-all of our existence; whereas they are only cogs in the wheel, or, better still, but jewels in the one great movement. The aim of politics, the aim of humanity, should be to have a Good Time. That is my re-religion. That is what I think we are here for. To have a Good Time. That's why I lost that train.

"I, sir, am a Hedonist, but I don't suppose you know what that means. It means having a Good Time. Doing what you like. Losing train after train if you want to lose them. Draining life to the lees." He dropped a walnut, and stooped to grope for it under the seat; while from his twisted body came more muffled words.

"What is it What's-his-name says? 'Hence, loathed Melancholy, of Thing-me-jig—where's that beastly nut?—of What's-his-name and blackest Midnight—got it!—born.' " He returned to the perpendicular with a grunt and took me by the lapel once more.

"A true Hedonist, you might say, would have let that nut lie. I beg to differ. The possession of that nut was of more importance to my happiness than the energy expended in stooping for it. You see, I am a vegetarian, and all the greengrocers are shut. A vegetarian, and a teetotaller."

He glared at me, and took hold of some more of my coat. " 'A teetotaller,' I said, young man." He was very fierce about it, so I agreed with him. Nor had I any evidence to the contrary. His speech was perfect, his ideas admirable; all except that about the losing of trains. But you must admit there were some grounds for my unexpressed doubts.

He threw a nutshell after the stationmaster's cat, who prowled the platform.

"There is perfect happiness," he said, and certainly the cat was having a Good Time with the nutshell; patting it, chasing it, leaping over it, and pretending to lose it. "That cat has absolutely no thought beyond enjoying herself. She is the complete Hedonist. Whitman has it. 'They do not lie awake in the dark and weep for their sins,' he says; and they have no trains to lose.

"But look at you! From twenty to fifty you spend your days grubbing for the means to enjoyment, forgetting—there's the signal— forgetting your object in the heat of the pursuit. And when you've got enough to buy the rose garden, the house, the ease of your heart's desire, you find that you have forgotten how to live. Dry toast and hot water will be your portion. Not your fault, of course. The whole scheme of things is wrong, rotten ... I wonder if that was the last train.

"For most of us life is like a—like a pomegranate—mostly pip. That is wrong. We are born too young; that's the trouble. In the perfect world, we should be born old, physically old, I mean. Somewhere about eighty; and get gradually younger until—well, of course, it's only an idea, and I haven't completed it yet. But you see the point? By the time you've saved a nice little competence, you'll be thirty." He began to get enthusiastic. "Think of it. Thirty, and full of life. Houseboat on the river, week-end bungalow, golf, cricket, travel; such a time! Then, of course, in another fifteen years you'll be getting too young for that sort of thing, and you'll go in for model engines, and so on. And so you will dwindle to five, three, two, one; and then—the thing begins to get a bit hazy there. Wants thinking out. 'Mr. So-and-So, the well-known banker, died yesterday at the ripe young age of three weeks. For some days the deceased gentleman had been unable to take his bottle.'

"It's a fine idea, though I admit there are flaws in it. Teeth, for instance, and shaving. A baby would look such a fool with a beard. I must think it out." And he returned to his walnuts.

Still, while I cannot but admire his views, and the universe as he would have remoulded it, I am a little doubtful of his teetotalism. Perhaps he was only a beginner.

The Assault

The skeleton trees in the park stood sharp and black against the flame of the sunset that paled to a blush overhead; and in the soft twilight of the east a faint star flickered.

Above, in the magic light, floated a wisp of cirrus cloud, a feather tinged with blood; and the wet pavements were mother-o'-pearl. And those that walked the pavements were bathed in the light, so that the street became a street of sweet thoughts, each face a benediction.

"A dear world," I said to myself, for a sweet content had entered into my soul; and I grinned hugely at the dying glow of the spent day. "A dear world and a dear people. Bless you, my children!"

Filled with such beautiful emotions, and for a while forgetting mundane things, I suddenly fancied a muffin, bountifully buttered. So I went into a tea-shop; a magic shop, from whose first floor casement I could watch the world wagging its tail, and see the motor-buses chasing the sun into the west. And the magic light played in the hair of the nymph who waited at the window for my order, clothed in the rosy effulgence.

Then came Tragedy and blew out the light, and darkened the world; so that my muffin was spoiled, and the nymph became just a waitress with dingy copper hair.

It was bad enough that the newcomer wore a dead fox round her neck. It was worse that she talked, in a voice to shatter dreams, of a Horror that had come to her that same afternoon. But I will tell you of the accident to poor Wimsey as she told it to her friend, and to the waitresses who giggled behind the tea urn, and to me, who, in my anxiety, put in three lumps instead of two.

First she placed Wimsey on a chair beside her, then laid on the table the parcel she had bought at the stores, her umbrella, gloves, purse, handbag, and bus ticket.

"If I don't positively have a cup of tea at once," she said, "I'm sure I shall absolutely collapse. *Such* an afternoon! My nerves!"

Her fingers pressed a spring concealed beneath her chin, and the dead fox opened its jaws, releasing his brush; and he, too, was laid on the table, a glass-eyed corpse staring at the menu.

"My smelling-bottle," said her companion, and rummaged in her bag. "It must have upset you dreadfully."

"My *dear* Charlotte! It was awful. *Awful*! I was never so thankful as when I caught sight of you. I'm sure I should never have got home." She turned to the chair on her left.

"Poor ickle Wimsey-Womsey then! Did the nasty man nearly kill him then?" She kissed the black snub nose of the Pekingese, and kissed it again and again. Then, remembering her desire for tea, rapped loudly on the table with the sugar tongs.

"We will have a pot of tea," she said, and the girl moved towards the counter. "For two," she added as an afterthought; but it did not reach the waitress, who came back to the table. "For two," was repeated, and again the girl started off.

The woman called her back with the sugar tongs. "China, Charlotte?" she asked. "It's so much more refreshing." Yes. China would do for Charlotte.

"Then a pot of tea for two; China," repeated the woman; and turned to feed Wimsey from the sugar basin.

"I never did like that commissionaire," she went on. "Nor did Wimsey, did you, pet? A brutal creature. I shall certainly write to the management about him, and threaten to take away my custom. A great, hulking brute." The tea arrived, and having arranged the table, the waitress left. But when halfway to the counter, the tongs called her back once more.

"Would you like some bread and butter, Charlotte? Or some pastries? Oh, I simply couldn't eat a mouthful. I'm that upset, you can't think." Then to the girl: "One of those what-d'you-call-'ems—

you know—pink, with the cream on top." The waitress trotted back to the counter. "And a meringue," added the sugar tongs.

"He ought to be discharged, you know; and I shall certainly see what a strong letter will do. You never saw anything so deliberate. I simply could not leave the pet in charge of such a creature again.

" 'You'll be careful of him,' I said, 'and not let him mix with the other dogs. And don't let him drink out of that trough,' I said; 'because he only has boiled water and milk at home.' Don't you, petsums?"

"And no sooner had I turned my back than I heard the darling cry. And there he was on his back, with that hulking brute bending over him." The meringue and the pink thing arrived.

"No, my dear Charlotte! I really could *not*." But Charlotte could; first the pink thing, then the meringue. You could see it was not her dog.

"He had struck the precious; knocked him down, in fact. Do you know, I spent half an hour trying to find the managing director. He said the wee thing had snapped at him. And you know, Charlotte, that Wimsey never snaps, except in play. I expect the darling wanted a romp. Did he den want to play with the nasty man?

"And the medals he wears! A man who has seen so much active service (if they really *are* medals, mind) could not help being callous and hard. And he called the pet a simply awful name, my dear! Have another meringue? Oh, do." She looked towards the tea urn and coughed loudly. Then coughed more loudly. "How does one call these girls?" she asked; and rediscovered the sugar tong method.

"One other meringue, and one other pink thing. Oh, yes! I'm sure you can, my dear. It's quite a time since lunch. One meringue, and one pink thing."

Like a dutiful maid the waitress dropped down the twenty-three stairs to the meringue and pink thing department, and clambered up again for the third time.

"I feel ever so much better after that cup of tea," the voice went on. "I really don't think I could have dragged along another step. But I shall never shop there again, all the while that brute is in charge of the dogs. I must speak to Charles about it. He knows a brother of one of the directors, you know. A scandalous thing, wasn't it, Wimsey, love?

"Yes. I think I could." Another tattoo from the tongs. "Will you fetch me an éclair? A chocolate éclair … And do you know, I've often given that man tuppence. Often! And then as soon as my back was turned—my dear! I knew the wee thing was in pain at once. No, only one lump this time. He did cry out so, didn't you, Wimsey?"

Does that sort of thing make the blood rush to your head? I wanted to address this woman in a loud voice. But she was feeding Wimsey with the éclair, and the waitress was leaning against the counter getting her breath. A hundred and eighty-four steps in nine minutes, and the bill would be a shilling.

But I kept quiet as long as I could, and then I was forced to speak.

"Madam," I said to my muffin in a low voice; "Madam, must you kill a waitress every time your lap-dog gets a clout? Must you—bah!" I said to my muffin, and stuck a fork into it. But it was cold, like the sunset; rigor mortis had set in. So I left for the dark street, and found that day had burned itself out, leaving but a few pale sparks drifting across the velvet sky.

The Sceptic

Like the Needy Knife-Grinder, I never love to meddle with politics. One gets so hoarse, and makes more enemies than converts. But with Mr. Abel Bullock it is different. I cannot get hoarse with him, and to make an enemy of him is impossible. He doesn't give one time.

A great man is Mr. Bullock, the pride of Lincoln Green, the chairman of its debating society, and the skip of its quoits club. Further, he is a member of the Royal and Ancient Society of College Youths; and once upon a time, before his waistcoat grew beyond all reason, he had stood to the five ton tenor bell of St. Alphege-under-the-Willow, and swung it without a sign of exhaustion through a set of Cambridge Grandsire Triples.

He often talks about it; more often than not.

But it is as a debater that Mr. Bullock most shines. Down at the sign of the "Little John" they will show you the dent in the counter with which he settled for all time the fiscal policy of the country. There is the mug, too, with which he made the dent, only now it holds a little less than the original imperial pint.

He prides himself on his open mind, does Mr. Bullock, and except for an explosive "Bosh!" or "Rot!" at half-minute intervals, he invariably listens to what his opponents have to say.

"Dogmatise" is another favourite word of his. "I'm as open to correction as any man," he will tell you, "and while not wishing to dogmatise, I say that what you're saying is nothing but a pack of lies. Don't tell me! I don't *think*. I KNOW! And that settles it. So shut up."

Should you persist, he falls back on his Grandsire Triples. "What's a jolly old market gardener know about Mexico? Tell me that! Stands to reason that a man what's gone through over five thousand tallies at change-ringing ought to know what he's talking about. And with the tenor bell and all."

A few nights ago the local ghost was under discussion; a noise, and a mysterious light that appeared at intervals in the upper windows of the Big House, long empty and of sinister repute. Little Toomey, the shoemaker, had seen it, years ago; and had gone headlong down the hill into the sheepwash. His conversion from Atheism dates from that night.

The pork butcher had also heard something, but he was not sure whether it was in '84 or '94. Something like a woman in pain it was, and yet somehow it wasn't. Like a pig being stuck, only muffled. More like a pig, perhaps, than a woman; and it was the same year that the big elm came down and nearly killed old man Potteridge.

Not being gifted with the eye of faith, I had asked Mr. Bullock for his opinion. He was fine! First he stabbed the fire to death with his walking-stick.

"Bosh! Tommy Rot!" he said. "There ain't no such thing. Ghostes!" And he kicked the spittoon across the room.

"Let me tell you that when a man's dead, he's dead and done with. No gallivantin' round empty houses; no trapesin' through churchyards. When a man's dead, he's DEAD! And the man what tells me different, tells me I'm a liar to my face. Ghostes!"

"But—" I began.

"Nothing of the sort, I tell you," said Mr. Bullock. "I refuse to believe in 'em. There ain't no such thing, so there!"

"But surely—" I interrupted.

"Don't you 'but' me," bellowed Mr. Bullock. "Don't you do it. I'm a plain man, and I look at the question from a logical point of view. When a man's dead, he's DEAD, so there! Has anybody ever caught one? No! And I refuse to believe in 'em. That's logic, ain't it? That's common sense."

"But supposing—" I ventured.

"Supposing!" snorted Mr. Bullock. "I won't suppose nothing. I know what I know. There ain't no such thing. And if you brought one here now, I'd tell him so. 'You're a hallucy—a thingmebob,' I'd say. So there!"

"But hearing's believing, ain't it?" asked the landlord.

"No, it ain't," thumped Mr. Bullock. "I can hear you, but I don't believe you. That's logic, ain't it? I tell you, one and all, I've read up on the subject. I've read a book on physicology, and that other stuff—what's-its-name—and I don't believe a word of it, so there!"

I felt somehow that I was getting the worst of things, so tried again.

"But surely—" I said.

"Don't you argue with me," yelled Mr. Bullock. "I *know*! It's flying in the face of reason. I put it to you as man to man. Do you, or do you not, believe in ghostes?" I was afraid I had no settled opinion on the matter.

"No opinion!" shouted Mr. Bullock with the help of his mug. "No opinion! After all I've told you. Where's your brains, man? Where's your intelligence? Why don't you use 'em? I tell you that when a man's dead, he's DEAD, and that settles it, don't it?" He drank long and deep, coming to the surface after a few minutes to splutter "Bosh!"

"I like a fair discussion," he went on, "and I'm proud to say that I'm open to be convinced. You can only get at the truth by argument. But ghostes! And groans! Don't it stand to reason that a man's got to have lungs before he can groan? Don't it? Of course it does. Don't you talk to me! Lungs, it's got to have."

"But surely—" I began.

"I won't hear another word," said Mr. Bullock. "Did you ever hear of a ghost with lungs? A ghost what breathed? Of course you didn't. Ghostes, I tell you, is just flimsy what's-'is-names, like puffs of steam. No bones or flesh or nothing. Visions, that's what they are. What you could walk through. Flimsy visions. Everybody knows that. And I say there ain't no such thing."

"But surely—" I interposed.

"I can't stop to listen to you," said Mr. Bullock. "It's a waste of time. You've made up your mind, and nothing won't shift you. Reason and logic and argument's no good when a man's made up his mind. Forty years I've lived here, man and boy, and I've never heard such a parcel of rubbish as you do talk."

173

"You can't get over that question of the groans. And the lungs. It's *got* to 'ave lungs to groan. That's common sense. It ain't *got* lungs. That's fact. Therefore it can't groan. That's logic. And I tell you there ain't no such thing, so there!" Mr. Bullock emptied the match stand into his pocket, and prepared to go.

"But surely—" I began.

"I tell you there ain't," panted Mr. Bullock. "And if I say there ain't, there ain't; so shut up."

"But surely—" I interrupted.

"Bosh!" said Mr. Bullock, and slammed the door.

The Peacemaker

I forget what my hurry was about now, but I was doing great things with the 100 yards record. Whether I was keeping an appointment or dodging one I have not yet been able to recollect; but I was doing it very well.

There was no sound in the quiet road but the clatter of my feet coming back from the houses opposite. Once or twice I caught a glimpse of an agitated window curtain, and a little boy called "Fire!" and ran alongside me for a while. But I put in my second speed and soon left him behind.

Then came disaster. I took a sharp corner on two wheels, as it were, and saw before me a girl with a jug, walking backwards, as is the custom of girls with jugs when you are running towards them. I made windmill motions with my right arm, but could not succeed in turning quickly enough.

There she stood with the jug, and in a second there she sat, the shards of the dismembered utensil strewed about her.

A little girl in tears is always a pathetic sight; but when that little girl is bawling on the ground, with bits of jug all round her (and maybe underneath her, too), it becomes yet more pathetic. Hers were melodious tears, tuned to attract attention; and every moment I expected a crowd with a policeman at its head to ask me, "Now, then, what's all this about?"

I picked the girl up, and recalled to my comfort the old nursery adage, "If you can squall like that, you're not hurt much."

"Clum—clumsy 'ound!" said the girl through her tears; then looked at the shapeless vessel on the pavement, and howled afresh. She leaned her arm on a municipal lamp-post, and her forehead on her

175

arm, and drooped like a wind-stricken daffodil, while the salt drops pattered about her feet like summer rain.

I put my fingers into my ticket pocket. It is a sad thought that a child crying suggests only pennies; our ideas of comforting the afflicted go no higher. But that was no good. I stood there like a fool, and could think of nothing to do.

"There, there!" I said. "Don't cry. Crying won't help matters. Let's see what we can do."

"Clumsy 'ound!" said the girl, and dabbed at her eyes with her pinny. "I shan't 'alf get in a row, I shan't. Far—farver won't 'alf go on, 'e won't." Then came inspiration. If father was going to do any going on he should go on at me. I struck my chest. I would see him and take the blame. The jug's blood be upon my head.

She brightened up at this, and helped me to kick the tinkling remnants into the gutter.

"Busted the set, that 'as," she said. "What my aunt give us, with blue geraniums on 'em. Three, there was. There's only two now. Farver won't 'alf go on, 'e won't."

"Wipe your eyes," I said, "and lead me to him." And so we started to seek out and mollify father. We walked in a silence broken only by occasional snuffles. Then I asked, "Would your father thrash you?"

"No, 'e wouldn't," said the girl. "Mother wouldn't let 'im. But 'e'll clout me, an' mother 'll clout me, too, an' they'll buy anuvver jug out of my elephant." Perhaps father would clout me instead, I thought, and asked how far it was to home.

" 'Bout ten minutes' walk, an' farver won't 'alf be wild, 'e won't. Busted the set, you 'ave. What'll you say to him?" I began to wish the way were longer. This was a case for diplomacy. Perhaps—I might dodge up that side street, and do some more running.

Perish the thought! Run away and leave the girl to her enraged father, and perhaps be pointed at one Sunday in a crowd, with "There's the man what busted the set, farver."

No; it must be faced out. But what sort of a man was father?

" 'E's a boilermaker." Dear, dear! A boilermaker. Big?

"Bigger'n you, lots!" This was becoming exciting. Could boilermakers run? Were they, as a class, light on their feet? I hoped not.

"An' I don't want to get in anuvver row," continued the girl; "because I got in a row last week, an' 'e clouted me. I poured some water in 'is eu-euphonium, an' it still plays a bit bubbly; an' farver, 'e's in the Prize Band, an' 'e wasn't 'alf wild, 'e wasn't. Caught me such a one-er, 'e did!"

We must be very near home now, and the job of explaining the accident to a boilermaker who was bigger'n me, and played the euphonium, did not look inviting. I must temporise.

"What time does your father get home?" I asked.

"He's always 'ome about now," said the girl. No hope there. "What you goin' to say to 'im?"

"Oh," I said lightly, "I shall just say I ran into and knocked you down," I answered.

" 'E won't 'alf be wild, 'e won't," said the girl. "If 'e goes to clout you, you dodge downwards, 'cos 'e's big an' tall." We were walking very slowly now. I had never met a furious boilermaker whose set of jugs with blue geraniums had been bereaved. A boilermaker's clout, I should think—never mind! I was in for it. Lead on.

The tears were all gone now, and the girl was beginning to look forward to the coming interview with an unholy glee.

"If 'e clouts you, what'll you do?" she asked.

"I don't think he will," I said. "But if he does, I shall—I shall—er—clout him back."

"Coo!" purred the girl. "You ain't seen my farver, you ain't. You couldn't reach." I liked it less and less. "It was the biggest one of the set, too!" she added. "The three-pint one. 'E won't 'alf be wild, 'e won't. An' my muvver, too!"

I liked the boilermaker's wife less than the boilermaker. Perhaps I might find a policeman to go with me. In any case I could open negotiations from the pavement with the front garden gate closed.

I could crouch in a sprinting attitude, on my toes, with my fingers lightly touching the ground in front of me; and start with, "Excuse me,

Mr. Boilermaker, but what will you have to drink?" and so on. The thing was preying on my mind.

Then I saw the china shop, and my health came back to me. Confound the boilermaker! Who was he, anyway?

That for him and his paltry jugs with the blue geraniums! There they were, hanging in the window, only the geraniums were pink.

I was not going to bandy words with a euphonium player, a coarse and brutal maker of boilers. Pooh! What was one jug to a member of a Prize Band? He should have his jug. Nay, he should have a complete set of jugs—the pint, the quart, and the three pints. I took the girl into the shop and bought them for her—one and sixpence ha'penny, and "Ain't you comin' round to see farver?" she asked.

"No," I said. "I am not. But you can give him my compliments. Mr.—er—Mr. Brown, of—er—Hammersmith's compliments, and he hopes the jugs will suit. Good-night!"

You never saw such a disappointed little girl as that boilermaker's bloodthirsty daughter.

The Goose

"Few things," says the tear-off calendar, "will gather a man's friends around him so quickly as adversity." The remark is attributed to Heine, but you cannot trust these tear-off calendars. Neither the sentiment nor the literary style reminds me of Heine a little bit. My opinion leans towards Confucius or Mr. Dooley. This by the way.

I have recently had it borne in upon me that this remark is true, in spots. Sometimes it comes off. Watch a man having a fit. See how his friends crowd round him, one to each button; two to his collar stud; one to yell for more air; another for more brandy.

Not that such willing helpers are always friends. I knew a man who had a fit in the City at the junction of Lime-street and Billiter-street. He lost his watch. As he remarked afterwards, it was a rotten fit, but a very good watch.

My recent example of the pseudo-Heine tear-off calendar platitude happened on Tuesday last. Of course, there was the Christmas influence in the air; but I should not like to think that my fellow creatures would not have rallied to the assistance of the afflicted one on January 25 or even February 25.

The central figure of the disaster that was the beginning of all things was a nervous little man with mutton-chop whiskers and circular spectacles. From his appearance I judged his name to be either Montmorency or Buggins; something silly, anyway; and I should think he was an Egyptologist by profession. He looked like an Egyptologist.

Like everybody else on Tuesday night, he was carrying parcels, four of them; a square box of bon-bons, a round box of Camembert cheese, two pairs of grey socks, and a mechanical toy. How do I know? Because he fell downstairs.

Eight men, two boys, and a railway policeman dashed to his assistance, picked him up, brushed him down, retrieved his cheese, and put his hat on straight; while he kept blinking and saying: "Thank you very much, it's nothing at all. I'm quite all right. It doesn't matter. Thank you very much."

Just as I was leaving the little crowd the nervous man let out a yell. "Oh, my goose!" he said shrilly, and we flew to his aid again, took his arms, and got him into the train.

"My goose!" he repeated, and putting the cheese and the socks and the bon-bons beside him, unpacked the mechanical toy. Feverishly he wound the key that stuck from under its wing. Then put the tin goose on the floor and watched it, eager-eyed. Nothing happened.

"It ought to walk," he said pathetically, and his eyes through the circular glasses looked big with tears. "It ought to walk. It walked in the shop all right."

"Lend it to me a minute," said the man in the next seat. "Perhaps we can put it right." He also wound it, and placed it on the floor. But, like a goose, the thing would not move. Just stood still and stared.

The willing helper shook it, and put it to his ear. "Nothing loose," he said; shook it again, and peered into its intestines. The nervous little man, Montmorency or Buggins, looked on with wide eyes.

"Let's have a go," said a man opposite, and he also shook it and listened. "That there thing ought to be round that there wheel," he said presently. "Got a penknife, anybody?"

A gentleman who looked like a lawyer produced a wonderful piece of cutlery, complete with two blades, a file, an awl, a nut-cracker, a corkscrew, a glass-cutter, and a hook; which last, when I had such a knife, was supposed to be used for getting stones out of horses' hoofs. But in those days I had no horse, and never got a chance of testing that part of the apparatus.

"Let me try," said the lawyer, and took the goose from the other. Now we all crowded round, while the amateur mechanic probed the animal's internal economy with the awl. Something clicked, and the nervous man, Buggins or Montmorency, leaned forward hopefully.

"If I could get that over there, and this bent straight," said the lawyer, "I think it would go all right." He prodded some more, then took off his hat. "Come up!" he said to something inside. "Ah, would you?"

"It walked all right in the shop," said Buggins. "And wobbled its neck," he added, after a little while. The lawyer was damp about the forehead now, but his blood was up. He leaned over to catch the light, and his glasses fell off. Without a word he picked them up and cleaned them, holding the goose between his knees.

"Now then! Got it! No. Got it! Confound it, it's slipped again. Now then, come up." He turned the key, and put the bird on the floor. There was a ten-second whir, and the goose fell sideways.

"I've done something to it anyhow," said the lawyer. "It didn't even buzz before."

"Let's have a look at it," said another of the audience, a man with a bag. "I'm an electrician, and know something about these things."

We passed the toy on to this new expert. He, too, stared long into its gizzard.

"That's bent," he said, "and that ought to go over there." From his bag he produced a narrow screwdriver, and got to work, a semicircle of heads bent round him.

"It walked all right in the shop," sighed Buggins, plaintively. "And wobbled its head from side to side. Very lifelike, it was." His eyebrows were trying to meet the roots of his hair.

"P'raps it wants oilin'," suggested a man with a basin tied up in a red handkerchief. "Them things wants a lot of oil. German it is, ain't it? Rotten workmen, them Germans. You try some oil."

Suddenly the goose gave vent to a prolonged "B-rrrrr!" and its legs moved rapidly. "Ah!" said its owner, and nearly fell off his seat.

"I think that's shifted it," said the electrician. "But it's a toughish job. Can't get at it, you know. If I had it at home on my bench, I'd put it right in two shakes. But I think it'll walk now all right."

"It walked in the shop," said the little man. "Up and down the counter, quite naturally. And wobbled its head just like a real goose."

"It's the rachet's gone wrong," said the electrician. "The pawl's slipped back, and doesn't catch when the spring's wound. If I can—get over!—if I can only—ah, you brute!—only get that back there—that's it! There! Now it ought to be all right."

He wound it up once more, and put it on the floor; and, wonder of wonders, it walked. It waddled from side to side, up and down the carriage, treading, like Agag, delicately.

"There you are!" said the electrician, full of pride.

"Th—thank you, very much!" said the nervous little man. "That's wonderful, really. But—but—I don't like to grumble, but you know, in the shop, its head wobbled like this, and it doesn't wobble now. D'you think—? It really ought to wobble. Like this, you know."

The electrician picked up the bird again. "Head wobbled, did it? Um! Then I think—"

"Don't you think that ought to go over there?" asked the lawyer. "It looks to me— Eh?"

"No!" said the electrician. "I reckon that works on that. See? And that thing does the wobbling. Now, if I can—" The screwdriver got to work again.

"Course, being an electrician, you'd know," said the man with the pudding-basin; "but I think the 'ead's joined on to the legs, an' the what's-its-name's busted. That's why she don't wobble."

The electrician rummaged in his bag.

"I want a thingmejig. You know, a long, thin thing that'll shove that connecting rod over, so! See?"

Five penknives, a fountain-pen, and a hair-pin were offered him by the audience, to which I contributed a collapsible button-hook. He took the hair-pin.

A tense five minutes while he jabbed at the bird's windpipe. We were all itching to get hold of the thing and take it to pieces; because we were all quite sure that if only that were put over there, and that bent straight, the goose would waddle and wobble as of old.

But we also realised the superiority of the electrician. He had made the halt to run up and down the carriage. Why should he not also make its neck wag?

"No go!" he said presently. "It won't come off. There's a thingumybob broke, and it'll never wobble any more. But it walks all right." He wound it up once more, and demonstrated that it would walk.

Said the Buggins man, "It walked all right in the shop, and wobbled its head from side to side, like this. D'you think the what's-its-name might have got caught in the ratchet?"

"No, it's broken!" said the electrician. "She'll walk all right, but her neck-wobbling days are over." He handed the bird to its owner.

"But it wobbled in the shop all right," sighed Montmorency, and gathered his parcels about him.

"I'm very much obliged to you," he said presently, as the train slowed up. "Very much indeed. I'm glad it walks again. I was afraid, when I fell down, and you all so kindly helped me, that it was damaged beyond repair. But thanks to you—if only you could have made its neck wobble! Good-night, and thank you all."

When he had gone we found his Camembert cheese under the seat, and the electrician put it in his bag. He said he was going to take it to the Lost Property Office.

The man with the basin in the red handkerchief said he *didn't* think.

Checklist of Issue Dates

The checklist below provides the original publication date in *The Star* for each of the sketches included in this collection.

"Bed and Breakfast," August 14, 1912.

"Of Saturday," October 5, 1912.

" 'This Style'," October 12, 1912.

"Going a Journey," October 26, 1912.

"Muffins," November 9, 1912.

" 'The Best People'," November 16, 1912.

"The 'Wow-Wow'," November 23, 1912.

"The District Visitor," November 30, 1912.

" ' 'Oppy'," December 7, 1912.

"The Step Maid," December 14, 1912.

"The Legacy," January 4, 1913.

"Domestic Repairs," January 11, 1913.

"The War of the Roses," January 18, 1913.

"The Leather Boxes," January 25, 1913.

"The Blue Minuet," February 1, 1913.

"The Lamp-Post," February 8, 1913.

"The Feud," February 15, 1913.

"The Passion-Flower," February 22, 1913.

"The Spike-File," March 1, 1913.

"The Quarrel," March 8, 1913.

" 'Poddles'," March 22, 1913.

"The Mayflower," April 26, 1913.

"The Beacon Fire," May 3, 1913.

"The Story-Teller," May 10, 1913.

"The Shepherdess," May 17, 1913.

"The Lions," May 31, 1913.

"Ambition," June 7, 1913.

"The Omen," August 2, 1913.

"The Snob," August 19, 1913.

"The Gardener," August 16, 1913.

"The Flower Girl," August 23, 1913.

"The Stray," August 30, 1913.

"The Skivvy," September 6, 1913.

"The Accident," September 27, 1913.

"The Last Straw," October 4, 1913.

"The Prodigy," October 11, 1913.

"Bookworms," October 18, 1913.

"The Stranger," October 25, 1913.

"The Reformer," November 1, 1913.

"The Assault," November 8, 1913.

"The Sceptic," November 29, 1913.

"The Peacemaker," December 20, 1913.

"The Goose," December 27, 1913.

F. W. Thomas

An Appreciation

The first article by F. W. Thomas was published on October 28, 1905. "On Getting the Sack" was sold to the *Morning Leader*, a Liberal halfpenny daily founded in 1892 and published, along with the similarly radical *The Star*, from the newspaper's offices in Stonecutter Street, London, E.C.4. Other articles followed, and within a year Thomas had joined the editorial staff of the *Morning Leader*, working as a junior reporter under editor Ernest Parke, who was at the helm of both newspapers. In 1908 Thomas showed his editor a humorous sketch he had written, asking him what he thought of it. Although Parke deemed it unsuitable for publication, he recognised his gift for humour and encouraged him to keep at it. Notwithstanding this, Thomas' excellent sketches and articles continued to appear in the paper on a regular basis over the course of the next four years.

Thomas' fledgling journalistic career with the *Morning Leader* ended in 1912 when the title came under the ownership of the Cadbury family and was absorbed into the *Daily News* to form the new *Daily News and Leader*. The London evening newspaper *The Star*, the *Morning Leader*'s long-standing sister publication, was also purchased by the Cadbury family. In May of 1912 Thomas joined the staff of that paper in their new offices in Bouverie Street; his first article for *The Star* was printed on August 14 of the same year.

From the outset, Thomas was a frequent contributor to *The Star*, where he remained for over thirty years. During this time he wrote hundreds of humorous stories and sketches and a regular Monday column that was usually accompanied by the artwork of numerous *Star* illustrators.

Thomas' most famous collaboration in this vein was with the noted political cartoonist David Low. Their successful partnership resulted in the popular "Low and I" series which began in 1922 and lasted for five years. The many humorous articles they produced consisted of reports of their visits to a variety of locations in and around London. These included such places as the Monument, the Tower of London, Billingsgate Market, the Serpentine, London Zoo, Madame Tussauds and Sotheby's. The "Low and I" series spawned two books: *Low and I: A Cooked Tour in London* (1923) and *The Low and I Holiday Book* (1925).

It could be said that the success of the series rather obscured the fact that the two had a slightly uneasy relationship. On arriving at Fleet Street all the way from Australia (he was originally from New Zealand), Low had expected to be working on a national daily. Considering himself a genius, he was said to have been somewhat disappointed at his placement on a London evening newspaper. With Thomas nine years his senior and, as the native Londoner, very much taking the lead as regards their location-based assignments, a little of the tension due to their different backgrounds and personalities does come across in the "Low and I" sketches. But the marriage of their talents produced some fantastic work, and over the years they built up a genuine fondness for one another. When one was off sick or on holiday, the other would "hold the fort" by carrying on the feature alone until their return. Thomas himself had some artistic ability and would enjoy supplying his own quirky cartoons in Low's absence.

This highly successful series finally ended in 1927, when Low left to work on the *Evening Standard*. After Low's departure Thomas continued the feature for a few more years, teaming up with the *Star* artist who signed his work as "Gee."

Down the years, Thomas' work for *The Star* also included a varied selection of informal essays and feature articles. Among these latter were a memorable series of travelogues in which Thomas documented extended visits he made to Paris, New York, Chicago and South America. It was on the first leg of this last trip, the background to which I will discuss in more detail later on in this essay, that Thomas met Rudyard Kipling in January 1927.

By chance Kipling was sailing out of Southampton on the same ship as Thomas, the R.M.S.P. *Andes*, bound for Buenos Aires. The night before embarkation Thomas had got wind of the fact that Kipling would be on board, and wired his editor, as any good newspaperman would feel obliged to do. After they had set sail the next day, the purser informed Thomas that he had made a faux pas, in that Kipling preferred the public not to know when he was off on his travels. Thomas apologised to Kipling and, in so doing, broke the ice, with the latter assuring him that he need not worry (as he couldn't have known), and besides, in his profession he was meant to be on the lookout for anything considered newsworthy. The two went on to enjoy a number of conversations on their way across the Atlantic. Years later these discussions formed the subject of a memoir that Thomas published in *The Star* in 1936.

Having published the reports Thomas sent back about his South American trip in 1927, ten years later *The Star* commissioned him to write a series of travelogues about his visit to the U.S.A. in 1937. Thomas' candid observations on the cities of New York and Chicago were well received, and were followed up by a string of equally funny articles detailing his visit to Paris in August of the same year.

But despite the importance of his travel articles and collaborative work, the bulk of Thomas' output for *The Star* was in the form of humorous writings which, for the most part, appeared on a weekly basis. The F. W. Thomas "Saturday Short Story" was a staple of the paper for decades, prompting the author and journalist Gerald Gould to describe him as "the man who is Saturday"!

Thomas was a gifted writer, equipped with a vivid imagination, an ear for dialogue and an ability to view commonplace situations in a highly individual way. This last aspect was summed up perfectly by a critic writing in the *Saturday Review* in 1923: "The most ordinary incidents furnish him with occasions of tenderness and cheerfulness. Mr. Thomas is a friendly philosopher—he comforts."

His stories were indeed marked by their gentle wit, lightness of touch and incisive insights into what makes people tick. These qualities were apparent in the stories he wrote about everyday London life, whether they were meditations on people's habits when travelling on the Underground, tales of put-upon City office workers, or the series of comedies which featured his outrageous fictional creation "Pamela," a scatter-brained high society girl.

And then there were all those strange tales set in a faerie world of his own devising that for years proved popular with readers of *The Star*. Peopled with an endearing cast of elfin folk and magical beings, Thomas' delicate, whimsical tales of fantasy proved beyond doubt his incredible versatility as a writer.

Perhaps Thomas' most important work for *The Star* were his many rural sketches, which he used in part as a showcase for his obvious love of nature and deep affinity with the English countryside. Several of these tales featured recurring characters, verbose eccentrics such as Mr. Grindle the Cobbler, his fatuous neighbour Simpson, and a small army of innkeepers, hawkers, shopping ladies and railway porters. Through characters such as these, Thomas (who after all was a trained journalist) used his powers of observation to good effect, employing wry humour to comment on the habits and foibles of people in rustic settings. He would also utilise made-up place names in his stories; the localities described therein would therefore represent just about any part of the British countryside. This aspect helped to establish the universal appeal of his humour. It is these latter stories and sketches, in which Thomas, in his own quirky way, documents his many hikes across the rural landscape, be it Sussex, Devon, or elsewhere, that comprise the main body of his vast literary output.

His writings for *The Star* and *Daily News* in this vein were well represented in book collections of his work. Hundreds of Thomas' pieces for the newspapers were reprinted in various hardbound editions. These include the best-selling volumes *Extra Turns* (1917), which was reprinted several times, *Saturday Nights* (1923), *Cobbler's Wax* (1925) and *Windfalls* (1932). All of his books were well received, and met with widespread critical acclaim, as reviews in numerous periodicals at the time testify.

Perhaps the most high profile critique of one of his books was by J. B. Priestley, whose esteem for Thomas was evident in a favourable review he wrote about the collection *Week-Ends* (1925). An ardent admirer of Thomas, Priestley reflected on the appeal of his humorous sketches: "The tales and sketches are the thing. They all have good ideas, of the kind O. Henry would have made into short stories, and, what is more important, they have a personal humorous flavour, that drollery which is unanalysable like a flavour or a scent, on the telling. The phonetic spelling itself is a triumph of observation." Priestley also felt that Thomas should be taken seriously as a writer: "Writing of this kind needs something more than a comic fancy, it needs a man who keeps his eyes and ears open and has observation and memory at the service of his calling. It needs, in short, a serious writer. That, I think, is the secret of Mr. Thomas' success as a humorous journalist. He is seriously occupied with the business of writing. He gives his work, however light it may be, however extravagant, the flavour of literature. He is, like all successful humorists, a sober craftsman and a serious man."

These sentiments were in fact an echo of some of Thomas' own thoughts on his approach to writing. In a rare interview printed in 1924 in his local paper the *Chiswick Times*, Thomas offered the following insight: "Let me tell you, being humorous is anything but funny; it is one of the most serious things in life. Anyone can be serious because life itself is serious, and it is no use to sit down and be tragic because, again, all things in life are tragic, but being humorous is the most tragic thing of the lot. You have to swallow all your own beliefs and opinions about life in general and take up an entirely new personality. People come to the office to see me sometimes and are disappointed. I believe they have expected to see a man with a red nose and a humorous cast of countenance—a sort of cross between Harry Lauder and George Robey—and instead of that have found a serious-looking young gentleman. It takes quite a serious man to be a humorist. As proof of that we have Dan Leno, whose great ambition in life was to play Romeo, Charlie Chaplin desired to play Hamlet, and my great ambition is to write a really serious novel, to do some good in the world. But humour has become such an integral part of my life now that I doubt if I could do it."

Beyond the readership of the *Daily News* and *The Star*, some of his sketches and stories found an even wider audience when they appeared in magazines such as *Lilliput*, *Tit-Bits*, *John O'London's Weekly* and *The Passing Show*. Thomas also co-wrote a stage musical called "His Girl," which ran for two months at the Gaiety Theatre at Aldwych in 1922. This extra exposure went some way towards increasing his fame. And who knows if his popularity would have expanded even further had he accepted the offer of Lord Beaverbrook (owner of the *Daily Express* and *Evening Standard*) to switch allegiances and come work on one of his newspapers for a higher salary? It's interesting to note that his old colleague on *The Star* David Low did just that thing, whereas Thomas is said to have enjoyed turning Beaverbrook down!

Towards the end of his long career with *The Star*, Thomas increasingly focused his creative energies on writing poetry. Prior to this, many of his articles and sketches had contained a liberal sprinkling of playful songs and verses. But throughout the late 1920s and into the 1930s he contributed to the paper a quite impressive string of narrative, story-length ballads. Some of these humorous verses were later collected in the book *The Ballads of Barnacle Bill and Other Jingles* (1943).

In 1929 Thomas found a fresh forum for his delightfully lopsided view of the world when he began a new column in *The Star* called "News From Nowhere." Renamed "This Cock-Eyed World" (later "Cock-Eyed Corner") in 1937, this was a mixed bag of jokes, riddles, musings and overheard conversations. It appeared in *The Star* on a daily basis, and lasted into the early years of the Second World War, when the column, at least in part, took on a satirical tone. On a visit to Germany in August 1938, Thomas had seen with his own eyes the persecution of the Jewish population by Hitler's regime. In the early months of 1940, Thomas used the final entries in the "Cock-Eyed Corner" series to poke fun at the Nazi propaganda regime. He was particularly scathing of Goebbels and the lies perpetrated by German radio broadcasts.

The ridicule Thomas meted out in this column and other articles with *Star* caricaturist Fred Joss, taken together with his prominent position as a long-serving journalist on *The Star* and *Daily News* (two newspapers that for years had been critical of Hitler's rise to power and the whole Nazi ideology), led to Thomas being placed on the Nazi death list, in common with his former colleague, David Low.

"Cock-Eyed Corner" was gradually phased out in favour of other features. There were for instance the brilliant "At Home with the Militia" sketches he produced in partnership with *Star* artist Leslie Grimes in the days leading up to the outbreak of war. In each of these pieces Thomas and Grimes would "fall in" with the new recruits at a number of army bases and send back reports of military life that were both illuminating and funny at the same time.

Following on from this series, Grimes would continue to contribute his regular "All My Own Work" feature, which showcased his fine cartoons and artwork in *The Star* for many years. A First World War veteran who had served as an air pilot and infantryman, Grimes also achieved renown for being the only British newspaper artist to visit the Royal Air Force in France in the weeks prior to the Allied retreat at Dunkirk. His exclusive drawings for *The Star* were flown home courtesy of the R.A.F.!

Thomas' work with Grimes made way for what proved to be a longer lasting collaboration with the legendary Roy Ullyett, another outstanding *Star* artist famous for his work as a sports cartoonist. The dozens of inspired articles they produced together were conceived very much in the style of "Low and I" and entertained readers into the early years of the war. The series was cut short when Ullyett received his call-up papers, going on to serve in the R.A.F. before returning to newspaper work on being demobbed.

The first few months of the Second World War were a particularly prolific period for Thomas, even by his standards. Starting in November 1939 Thomas compered the "Stories of the Home Front" column. In this feature he invited readers to send in anecdotes relating to their experiences of home-made trenches, black-outs and air-raids.

This feature proved to be short-lived, however, and was ultimately superseded by a column that Thomas had much experience of writing. In addition to his prolific output for *The Star*, Thomas had conducted the long-running "Merry-Go-Round" column in the *Daily News* (renamed the *News Chronicle* in 1930) throughout the 1920s and 1930s. Not dissimilar to the "This Cock-Eyed World" column, this feature was supplanted to *The Star* during the Blitz of 1940. A fun-packed miscellany of jokes, trivia, puzzles and readers' letters,

"Merry-Go-Round" sadly fell victim to wartime restrictions on paper usage. As *The Star* itself shrank in page count, Thomas' column got smaller and smaller, until by the end of 1941 it had been phased out completely.

Among his very last contributions to *The Star* were the wartime sketches he wrote as part of the "From the Coastal Zone" series, which ran from 1941 to 1945. These humorous pieces told the story of everyday life in a small community on the Sussex Coast during the Second World War. The locale was obviously Thomas' hometown of Seaford in East Sussex, though for reasons of national security the exact location was not revealed at the time. This aspect would have come naturally to Thomas, as he had for years been apt to use made-up place names in most of his sketches and stories. The "From the Coastal Zone" series is of some historical interest today, detailing as it does the effect on a quiet seaside town of the sudden invasion of barracked troops, gun emplacements, barbed wire, food rationing and German air-raids. These unique and fascinating pieces remain highly readable today, over sixty years since they were originally published.

Thomas' final article for *The Star* appeared in November 1945. In "A Word to Mr. Wells" Thomas urged readers not to take all of H. G. Wells' predictions too seriously, arguing that while some had turned out to be accurate, others had not. Apparently the general mood of the nation at the time this article was written was one of gloom, and it's perhaps fitting that Thomas signed off from *The Star* by telling everybody to "cheer up"!

After his retirement from newspaper work, Thomas collaborated with *The Star* and *News Chronicle* illustrator James Francis Horrabin by contributing songs and verses for his "Japhet and Happy" cartoon annuals (he had previously written stories based on Horrabin's "Dot and Carrie" cartoon strip). From 1947 onwards Thomas worked as a book reviewer for the magazine *John O'London's Weekly*. His contributions to this periodical, which lasted until early 1953, also included several feature articles and the occasional humorous short story.

A very private man, throughout his long career as a Fleet Street newspaper journalist he was never given to talking much about himself. Hard biographical information about Thomas was rather thin on the ground, indeed virtually non-existent are far as his many readers at the time were concerned. Even at the height of his popularity, reviewers of his book collections would note that about the man himself, little was known to the public. One could glean certain odd snippets of information from his writings, and make educated guesses about just *who* F. W. Thomas the man was. Readers could infer his literary tastes (such as his fondness for Shakespeare and Keats), that he smoked a pipe, owned a dog, was a keen ornithologist, enjoyed long walks, country pubs, good conversation and was an eternally patient observer of people.

As for the biographical facts that we now know today, our knowledge of his early life is limited to scarce items of information. It is known that Frederick William Thomas was born in Hackney, London on January 14, 1882. His father was a merchant seaman who later worked as a fishmonger. His parents had several children, and although he grew up alongside his siblings in the family home in Hackney, both his maternal and paternal ancestral roots were centred in the Rye and Udimore districts of East Sussex.

Thomas attended a Board School in Hackney but left at the relatively early age of thirteen. An avid reader who was largely self-educated and had a good head for figures, as a young man he obtained work as an invoice clerk for a commercial concern in the City of London. Finding himself unemployed in 1905, he began submitting candid articles about his jobless plight to the *Morning Leader*. The editor did not hesitate to publish Thomas' wry and honestly written contributions, and within a year he had joined the paper as a clerk. Soon afterwards he secured a placement on the editorial staff of the *Morning Leader*. Interviewed in 1924, Thomas recalled the background to his joining the paper: "At that time I knew nothing about journalism, except that you must write on one side of the paper only and not split infinitives."

Around the time he joined *The Star* in 1912, Thomas got married and moved to Chiswick in West London. For 17 years Thomas commuted to the City from this suburb, where he lived with his wife

Louisa Augusta (nee Podbury) and their two children Margaret and Peter. Meanwhile, his writing career went from strength to strength.

The aforementioned trip that he made to South America, which resulted in several articles, had a background of personal tragedy. Thomas' son died in 1926 at the age of 11, and in January 1927, the proprietors of *The Star* and *Daily News* sent Thomas on sabbatical leave, while he came to terms with the loss of his beloved son. A news item in *The Star* was published on January 29, 1927, informing Thomas' many fans of his absence. The following extract reveals how important to the paper he was: "The fact is that F. W. Thomas has been getting a little bit under the weather, though you would never have suspected from his *Star* articles that he was what is commonly called 'run down.' Thomas will carry with him the good wishes not only of his colleagues, but of the many thousands of *Star* readers for his complete restoration to good health—and high spirits."

Ever the professional, Thomas had evidently been working through his grief, and one can surmise today that his fellow newspapermen on *The Star* and *Daily News* could see that both physically and mentally he was running himself into the ground.

On the orders of his editors, in late January 1927 Thomas boarded the R.M.S.P. *Andes*, setting off from Southampton on a sea voyage that would last several weeks and whose ultimate destination was Buenos Aires. It was on the trip across the English Channel to Cherbourg, during which Thomas had the previously discussed meeting with Rudyard Kipling, that he began to compose reports on his travel experiences, to be posted back to *The Star* at the next port of call. Continuing to write his letters home as the ship made its way across the Atlantic to Pernanbuco and then on to Rio de Janeiro and Montevideo, Thomas' entertaining missives began to appear in *The Star* in March of that year. Published while he was still away under the heading "Chasing the Sun," the articles he sent back described his long train journey across land from Buenos Aires to Valparaiso in Chile, and from there his second sea voyage aboard the R.M.S.P. *Oropesa*. Stopping off at various ports on the coast of Peru, this second vessel eventually brought Thomas through the Panama Canal and across the

Caribbean Sea via Jamaica, Havana, and finally Bermuda before re-crossing the Atlantic and arriving at Plymouth in early April.

His odyssey to South America having taken over two months, Thomas returned to the pages of both papers in April 1927. In somewhat sporadic fashion, David Low had continued the "Low and I" column in his absence. Thomas wasted little time in teaming up again with his long-term colleague, while over at the *Daily News*, he resumed his weekly "Merry-Go-Round" feature, which Ashley Sterne had ably conducted while he was away. With his customary "Saturday Short Story" appearing every week, a revitalised Thomas was back on form in no time.

Two years later the pull of his family heritage proved too strong to resist, and in 1929 he and his wife relocated to East Sussex; a region where he spent the remainder of his days. Writing from his home on the South Downs, he regularly sent in his copy to the London offices of *The Star* and *Daily News*, occasionally dropping in to the Bouverie Street headquarters on visits to London.

Facts such as these, however, would not have been revealed to his readers at the time. What was known of Thomas as a journalist and humorist far outweighed the knowledge they would have had of his personal life, particularly in the final years of his career with *The Star*. To such an extent, in fact, that after his last piece appeared in a November 1945 issue of the paper, to the public at large, no more was heard of Thomas. True, if one happened to read *John O'London's Weekly*, or see his name on Horrabin's "Japhet and Happy" annuals, one would have been aware of his post-war output. But neither *The Star* nor the *News Chronicle* carried any announcements of his retirement and certainly no acknowledgement whatsoever that his long newspaper career had come to an end. Back then, his faithful readership on the paper would have been left wondering what had happened to him. It should be noted, though, that all this mystery was admittedly in keeping with the author's long-standing and carefully maintained privacy.

From my own point of view, having discovered his work so many years after he was famous, for a long time I pondered on the mystery of what had become of Thomas after 1945. This enigma lasted until very recently, when a genealogical researcher friend of mine managed to uncover various items of vital biographical information, such as his date of birth. And then, by coincidence, shortly after this I was contacted by Thomas' grandchildren, who acknowledged certain facts already guessed at and revealed much more relating to his life after 1945.

Thomas lived out much of his retirement at his home in the East Sussex seaside town of Seaford, where he had lived since 1929. After his wife died in 1961, he finally settled with his daughter's family in the village of Old Heathfield. During the remaining years of his life Thomas served as honorary treasurer of the Searchlight Cripples' Workshops in Newhaven, an organisation partly aimed at helping disabled war veterans. He remained an avid reader and enjoyed gardening, archaeology, wildlife and sitting in his greenhouse, thinking and dreaming away the hours. Thomas was immensely fond of his three grandchildren and was apt to entertain them with his poems, cartoons, and beautifully constructed models of villages, complete with ponds, churches, and hedges, etc.

Much loved by all of his family, he passed away at his home aged 84 on October 3, 1966. Among those who attended his funeral was Arthur Webb, an old colleague from *The Star*. Obituaries for Thomas were printed in *The Times* and his local paper the *Sussex Express*.

And so the biographical information and insights kindly supplied by Thomas' grandchildren now help to shape our understanding of his autumn years. With this newly acquired knowledge, one can only hope against hope that the day will come when more readers will discover the brilliant works of this talented writer. His legacy of varied writings is surely long overdue for a revival.

For now, I offer to the modern reader these new collections of his work, bringing F. W. Thomas' unique brand of humour and observational talents into the light once again.

Richard Simms
Surrey, England
February, 2010

Further Reading

The long career F. W. Thomas had with *The Star* is discussed in more depth in the essay "F. W. Thomas: Star Man," published on the internet at the following web address:

http://thestarfictionindex.atwebpages.com/f_w.htm

The same website also contains a comprehensive checklist of the short stories and fictional sketches Thomas contributed to *The Star* from 1912 through 1945.

www.ingramcontent.com/pod-product-compliance
Lightning Source LLC
LaVergne TN
LVHW011228080426
835509LV00005B/391